Be Your Mate's Best Friend

Be Your Mate's Best Friend

by

Stephen & Janet Bly

MOODY PRESS

CHICAGO

© 1989 by
STEPHEN AND JANET BLY

All Scripture quotations, unless noted otherwise, are from the *New American Standard Bible,* © 1960, 1962, 1963, 1968, 1971, 1972, 1973, 1975, and 1977 by The Lockman Foundation, and are used by permission.

ISBN: 0-8024-3576-9

1 2 3 4 5 6 Printing/BC/Year 93 92 91 90 89

Printed in the United States of America

To Art & Alice:
Best friends for life

Contents

1

A Good Friend Is Hard to Find

I remember the first time I saw her.

It was the second week of September, 1958. She had long, shiny brown hair, teasing eyes, and pouting lips that at the time reminded me of a movie star. Rumor had it that she already had a boyfriend. It was just as well. I was too embarrassed to talk to her anyway. I had grown up in the country and felt much more comfortable with trees, animals, and tractors.

But my name being Bly, and hers being Chester, we were destined to sit next to each other in every class that had alphabetical seating assignments. In our freshman year that turned out to be Miss Menendian's English class.

Now I want to be the first to admit I was not the most cool dude at Redwood High School. I was a farm boy who had to travel to the city to go to high school. I was there with my flat top hair cut, blue jeans, white t-shirt, and black high-top tennis shoes. I was one of twenty-nine eighth grade graduates from Ivanhoe Elementary, many of whom chose to go on to high school.

By Christmas I still hadn't gotten up enough nerve to speak to this talkative young lady more than a few times. Little known to her, she had made my list of the ten cutest girls at Redwood High.

It took three more long years, and ownership of a 1955 Chevy convertible, before I took a chance and asked her out for a date. To my utter amazement, she said "yes." To my continual bewilderment, she is still saying "yes."

Back in 1958, at age fourteen, I had no idea in the world that this cute, young teen would some day be my wife. And I never, even in my wildest teenage fantasy, dreamed that she would also be my very best friend. But in the process of the last thirty years of discussion and over twenty-five years of marriage, we have built not only a family and a ministry but a friendship that has weathered the storms, struggles, sorrows, delights and joys of life. We are parents and partners, lovers and roommates—but providing the stability beneath all of those roles is the fact that we are best friends.

For the young or unmarried all of this might seem a bit routine. There is the notion abroad that things happen automatically. "People get married, and they become good friends because they live together and have to learn to get along."

So they say.

Wrong.

All the married folks we know either have a good growing friendship and know they have to be diligent in continuing to build it or it will crumble; or they have a lousy friendship and know something must happen soon or there will be nothing to hold them together.

Now it doesn't matter at all whether you have been married five years or fifty years—you need to keep working at building a friendship in marriage.

But some married folk are never friends. Why is it?

THREE REASONS WHY MARITAL FRIENDSHIPS FAIL

CONFUSING PROXIMITY WITH FRIENDSHIP

We have a tendency to convince ourselves that wedding vows and golden rings automatically produce friendship. That's like planting a hubcap and hoping to grow a Corvette. The close proximity of one human being to another does not automatically produce friendship.

Are you best friends with all those siblings who grew up in your own household? Maybe. Maybe not. Are you best friends with the roommate you had in college? Maybe. Maybe not. And are you best friends with the guy who has worked alongside of you all these years?

Maybe. Maybe not. It takes a lot more than being together to make a friendship.

Ask our friends Tony and Natalie. We had been counseling with them for over ten years. It was always one long series of complaints. No matter which one we talked with it was always the same. He "doesn't care about anyone but himself." She "is always too critical of me." "I can't take it anymore." "I shouldn't have to put up with this."

So after the kids grew up and moved out, after twenty-eight years of a bickering marriage, they've decided to call it quits. With the kids gone, there's nothing left of the relationship. They just don't like being around each other. They have little in common. Not only are they not friends, they are, indeed, worst enemies.

It's incredible. After almost thirty years of living in the same house, eating at the same table, sleeping in the same bed, and crying over the same problems, they never became friends. But Tony and Natalie are not unique. The scene is repeated over and over in every neighborhood.

UNDERVALUING FRIENDSHIP IN MARRIAGE

Many couples give friendship too low a priority in the marriage relationship. In describing the perfect marriage some rate finances as the most important. Others list sexual compatibility. Many strive for life-styles that harmonize. Some look for cultural and social similarities.

How about building friendship in marriage? "Oh," they say, "that's no big deal. You can develop a friendship with almost anyone."

Our friend Jerry was a fire captain in Phoenix. At forty-six years of age he succumbed to the fashionable trauma of having a mid-life crisis. All the pitch about faster cars, younger women, and freedom convinced him to abandon his wife and family. Jerry settled on a silver 300ZX, a condo in Scottsdale, and a gold chain around his neck. He dropped twenty pounds, took the grey out of his hair, and started wearing brightly colored surfing shirts.

It didn't take long before Jerry invited a young lady friend to move in with him. "She's not like Sarah," he told us.

He was certainly right about that. Sarah, his wife, was forty-five years old. She had borne him four children, one of whom had died after only six months of life. Sarah was at least fifteen pounds heavier than she had been at their wedding. The three kids were in their teens, which kept her extremely busy, especially now that she was raising them alone. She was smart, bright, attractive, and extremely capable, but she openly admitted to being too demanding at times.

But Jerry's lady friend was only twenty-three. She looked great in a bikini. She thought Jerry was "really neat." She liked driving fast in the open T-top, taking trips to Las Vegas, and dressing in slinky gowns. She clung to Jerry's arm wherever they went. "She is not at all like Sarah," he repeats.

Eleven days after his divorce became final, Jerry married his lady friend. Five weeks later he called us to announce it was all over. He just couldn't live with his new wife anymore.

That was last May. In June, Jerry came over to see us. He said he was on disability from the fire department. It seems they had gotten an emergency call and he had taken his crew to the wrong address. He got so flustered, he forgot what to do next. The department listed it as extreme stress. He began to describe the shallow relationship he had with his new wife and how much he missed Sarah. Of the new wife he said, "I can't even talk to her. We have nothing in common."

What he missed most of all was not Sarah's looks, not her charm in public, not her body. What he missed was her friendship. Jerry didn't have much of a problem finding a less grey and wrinkled physical partner, but he did have a problem trying to find someone who was as good a friend as Sarah. "I need to get a divorce and remarry Sarah," he told us.

But it was too late for that. Jerry should have weighed the high value of friendship a long time ago.

NEGLECTING THE BIBLE'S GUIDANCE

Friendships fail in marriage because far too many folks neglect the clear guidance of the Bible. According to the scriptural text, God created every man, woman, husband, and wife on earth. "And God created man in His own image, in the image of God He created him; male and female He created them" (Genesis 1:27).

Not only that, but it is God who instituted marriage. "For this cause a man shall leave his father and his mother, and shall cleave to his wife; and they shall become one flesh" (Genesis 2:24).

We are created by God as male and female. He initiated that special relationship called *family*. He charged us to be husband and wife. It seems reasonable that no one would know better than God how we are supposed to act in such a relationship and what we should expect to gain from it.

The lesson in Genesis is not aimed merely at faithful believers but at every person created by God. God's teaching holds true for all ages and all cultures and all circumstances.

It would seem logical to assume that those who choose not to believe in God would hesitate even to consider biblical teaching on any subject. Likewise, one would think that true believers—those who have discovered a personal commitment to Jesus Christ—would readily turn to the biblical texts for needed guidance in family matters.

Sadly enough, this isn't true. Tony and Natalie, Jerry and Sarah each claim to be a Christian, saved by the death of Christ on Calvary. Yet they foolishly rejected the guidance on marriage God provides in the Bible.

How does a person begin to understand such teaching? By learning to accept the basic roles God has established for a husband and a wife. Chapter 2 looks into those roles and how crucial they are in any marital friendship.

But for now, as we think at the trouble and destruction taking in place in family units these days, we would like to deal with a more basic question: "Why did God create us to live in families? Is that really the best plan? Couldn't He have figured out something better?"

FIVE BIBLICAL REASONS GOD CREATED THE FAMILY UNIT

COMPANIONSHIP

God created families for companionship. "Then the Lord God said, 'It is not good for the man to be alone' " (Genesis 2:18).

Man was created lonely. Men and women are social beings. We do not exist in the completeness of our humanity apart from other folks. In particular, we need especially the companionship of one particular mate. The opposite sex was created as proof of our incompleteness.

This is certainly a major reason for the creation of the marriage relationship, but perhaps not the most crucial. If the only purpose of marriage were companionship, then God could have supplied such companionship through another means. Perhaps each of us could have been given visual, audible contact with a personal guardian angel. Or God could have created us complete in the first place. It in no way stretches His ability to create a being that is totally content in isolation.

The fact that He chose not to do so indicates there may be a deeper reason for creation of the marriage relationship.

PROCREATION

God created families for procreation. "And God blessed them; and God said to them, 'Be fruitful and multiply, and fill the earth, and subdue it; and rule over the fish of the sea and over the birds of the sky, and over every living thing that moves on the earth' " (Genesis 1:28).

The marriage relationship was designed by God to populate the earth with people. It was His purpose that the sexual union of husband and wife would produce children who in turn would grow up and produce children of their own.

As absolutely vital as procreation is, it just might not be the most important reason the family unit was created. If God merely wanted a planet full of people, He certainly could have created them all at once. A God who merely spoke the word and millions of galaxies came into being, each filled with millions of stars, would have no trouble in creating five billion humans all at once.

Or couldn't He have created a type of being that reproduced itself without the help of a mate? That sounds like a strange scene from a cheap science fiction movie, but would not have been beyond the Lord's power. The point is, if merely preserving the species was His plan, God could have chosen other options. He stuck with marriage for a purpose.

MUTUAL ASSISTANCE

God created families for mutual assistance. "I will make him a helper suitable for him" (Genesis 2:18).

It is a great big world we live in. Even when it is compared to the greater size and magnitude of the universe, planet earth is more than one man can handle. Cultivating and keeping even a portion of it, as Adam found out in the garden of Eden, can be a tremendous burden. We need help.

We need the physical strength, the moral courage, and the emotional encouragement others have to offer. The marriage relationship can and should provide such assistance.

But again we must ask if that is the most important purpose of marriage. Couldn't those needs be met in a different way, perhaps through a special "helper" being? Such a helper could be strong, wise, caring, but unobtrusive, never nagging. You know—a little junior assistant always cheerfully doing all that we ask of him.

Or couldn't God have created us to be totally self-sufficient, not needing any help?

The point is, He didn't. We are created to be in a marriage relationship of husband and wife. Perhaps the most important reason is still yet to be found.

LEARNING ONENESS

God created families for learning oneness. "For this cause a man shall leave his father and his mother, and shall cleave to his wife; and they shall become one flesh" (Genesis 2:24).

Now we are getting to the heart of the matter. There is a mental, spiritual, and physical oneness in marriage that is unlike any other human relationship. Why is learning oneness so important? Jesus gave us the answer in John 17:21: "That they may all be one; even as Thou, Father, art in Me, and I in Thee, that they also may be in Us; that the world may believe that Thou didst send Me."

The ultimate expression of oneness is in the relationship between the Father and the Son. Mankind was created so that we might enjoy the fellowship of that kind of oneness. But how in the world will selfish man learn the benefits of oneness while he is still here on this earth? Through the experience of marriage.

Marriage is a spiritual arena in which to learn what it means to be one with another. Have you ever wondered why adultery and idolatry were so often lumped together in Scripture? At times they seem interchangeable. The people of Israel were accused of committing adultery, when, in fact, they had worshiped false gods—idolatry. Adultery and idolatry are often seen together because they are both a breaking of oneness. That is the most serious offense that can be committed. Idolatry is a breaking of oneness with God, and adultery is a breaking of oneness with your mate.

Marriage is the proving ground of oneness.

UNDERSTANDING CHRIST'S LOVE

God created families for understanding Christ's love. "Husbands, love your wives, just as Christ also loved the church and gave Himself up for her" (Ephesians 5:25).

Even a quick reading of the biblical teaching about home life in Ephesians 5 shows the continual parallel Paul makes between married life and Christ's role in the church. Of the twelve verses between Ephesians 5:22 and 33, he mentions Christ's role in the church in eight of them.

This, then, is the other main reason for marriage as God designed it: to be a daily object lesson in Jesus' love relationship with the church. If we fail to understand what the biblical roles for husbands and wives are, we will never properly grasp the deep affection Jesus has and the leadership he provides for the church.

Family life was designed for a spiritual purpose. Life on this earth is a training ground for the life to come. All of us need some preparation for eternity. For most folks on earth, being a husband or a wife is a central part of that preparation.

So where is a good place to begin? How about the obvious? Why not find out what your mate really wants in a friendship. Chances are you have never really sat down and discussed the subject with each other, no matter how many years you have been married. What you have learned has probably been through many trials and much error, but perhaps not through simple communication.

Grab a couple of notepads and pencils, sit down at the table, and write out a list of the ten most important qualities of a best friend. Maybe our lists will give you some inspiration.

JANET'S LIST: TEN THINGS I WANT IN A BEST FRIEND

1. *God is central in his life.* My best friend seeks God's will in the daily matters of living—through regular fellowship with mature Christians, consistent study of the Bible, and growth in his prayer communication. He seeks to understand his experiences and situations from a divine viewpoint. And he is always glad to pray for me in times of need. When I'm hard to live with, he remains faithful to me because of his commitment to the Lord God.

2. *He is a dreamer.* An exciting friend is one whose mind is active. He's always thinking, probing, planning, looking to the future, and making the present come alive. He despises boring ruts. He recognizes and willingly meets challenges that fit his gifts, temperament, and call from God. He also enjoys surprises, such as an overnighter at a beach resort, a fortieth birthday party; or simple things like picking up the dry cleaning or the groceries without being asked.

3. *He has a sense of humor.* Because I'm such a melancholy temperament by nature, I want and need to laugh. I need someone to help me see the lighter side of things. I enjoy humor that's a little wacky, good satire, and—best of all—dry wit, as long as it's not blasphemous or obscene. My best friend knows the boundaries between the topics that are sacred and the ones that are fair game.

4. *He shares with me a common interest or hobby.* I enjoy writing stories, poems, and songs of all varieties. I like camping in the woods, gazing at meteor showers, and studying geology. Some of my favorite activities include eating out at a restaurant that has character, traveling to out-of-the-way places, shopping for things you don't have to try on, and lying on a boat, beach, or deck to read. I expect my friend to have different experiences, and there's a good chance I'll acquire a few interests because of him. But we've also got to have some things we can both do together.

5. *He works at building our friendship.* It's no fun to be the one always doing the giving, and to get little or no response in return. I

should be able to see some changes taking place because he wants a better relationship, not merely because I'm nagging him.

6. *He's thoughtful, but not manipulatively generous.* I dearly love those touches of expression or gifts that say, "This made me think of you." But I feel uncomfortable if someone gushes over me or does more for me than I can reciprocate. When that happens, I feel guilty —and think I'm not as good a friend to him as he is to me.

7. *He loves me with touch.* Snuggles. Hugs. A stolen kiss in a suddenly empty K-Mart aisle while we are shopping. A knowing secret pat or a wink in a crowd. There's also the "touch-talk"—the secret language of two best friends—that asks, "Guess what I'm thinking about right now?" or "What color are the . . . ?" It includes the unexpected note—on a pillow or the bathroom mirror, stuck to the dash of the car, or received out of the blue in the mail.

8. *He openly admires a trait or ability of mine.* A friend affirms and encourages me through his words of appreciation. And he does so with utter sincerity and honesty. I can spot a mile away the flattery spoken for a hidden motive. But this friend treasures me as a person who is special and unique, vital to his existence.

9. *He doesn't put me down in public.* I do stupid things sometimes, especially when I'm having a good time with a group of friends. I get too talkative, silly. But my best friend waits until I get home to tell me to keep quiet or to correct my mistakes.

10. *He's patient with my femaleness.* I need a few more trips to the doctor than he does. There are days I don't feel so well, and I worry about all kinds of things—like being pregnant. (How many times have I gone through that routine?) I have a tendency to think I've contracted every new disease. I have storms because I want a child (or don't want a child). Sometimes I don't feel fulfilled or attractive or needed. Some days I need to be like a little girl and sit protected in someone's lap, or I need to find some activity that's just play. My best friend understands these things.

1. *I want a best friend who trusts in God.* That means she trusts Christ as her personal Lord and Savior. That means she trusts the Bible as His inerrant Word. My best friend does not have to be persuaded to study, worship, pray, and grow. She has a burning desire to please God daily and to accept where He is leading.

2. *I want a best friend who supports what I am doing.* I need someone who is constantly looking for ways to help me succeed. One who is busy making me look good. A friend who thinks my success is important. One who listens, counsels, and works alongside me, when need be.

3. *I want a best friend who will be loyal.* She will always be on my side. She will always be available to console me. Even the hint of unfaithfulness in her would sound absurd. She will be a friend who is in the relationship for the long haul of life. I can count on her always being there.

4. *I want a best friend who is transparent.* She will not be manipulative. She will not have hidden agendas for my life or hers or ours. She will be blunt rather than obscure. She will tell me honestly how lousy or how great she feels. She will give me her honest opinion, even if it crushes my dreams or images.

5. *I want a best friend who surprises me.* She breaks out of her pattern every once in a while and does something totally uncharacteristic. I like to discover that I don't know all there is to know about this person . . . that she has been secretly planning something for me . . . that there are still more treasures in her personality that I have not yet fully enjoyed.

6. *I want a best friend who is receptive to my strengths.* I can do some things well. I want her to appreciate those things and enjoy them. I want her to need me, to be proud of my strong points. I need someone to help me find a place where I am able to do the things that I do best.

7. *I want a best friend who calls me to account.* She has the strength to tell me I have gravy on my chin, my shirt doesn't match my jacket, and my story about the worms was way out of line. I want her to point out where my behavior varies from the biblical standard, when I am side-tracked from the Lord's leading, and when my methods don't measure up to my lofty goals.

8. *I want a best friend who has a sense of abandon.* I need her to be able to grab a coat and some boots and be ready to head to the mountains in ten minutes' notice. I want her to sense when it's extremely important to me for her to be with me. I want her to have a babysitter on the back burner so that, if necessary, she can be at my side at the drop of a cowboy hat.

9. *I want a best friend who is fun.* She can make me smile, change my attitude, and help me forget my struggles. She knows what makes me laugh, and she makes sure I have opportunities to do so. She takes the time to learn to enjoy some of the things that bring me delight. She can sit through a dusty rodeo with a smile on her face and a gritty hot dog in her hand.

10. *I want a best friend who challenges me to be my best.* She inspires me to be something. She thinks so highly of me that I push myself to excel just so I won't let her down. She knows the things that bring satisfaction to my ego, and she constantly encourages me to honestly achieve them. She refuses to let me be mediocre . . . or worse.

Now you are getting the picture.

Make your own lists. They might be similar to ours. They might vary quite a bit. When you have completed your lists, spend an evening talking about each point you have written down. Make sure you both understand what is being said and implied.

Your lists will be preliminary ones. The chances are that as you continue to study the whole idea of strengthening friendship in marriage you will redefine your lists. Yet don't pass up the opportunity to begin to become each other's best friends right now.

After you have discussed your lists, pick out three categories that at this moment in your life are the ones in which you need the most encouragement.

Share those three categories with each other and agree to begin this very week to strengthen your friendship in those areas.

Sure, it will take some extra thought and work. You might have to readjust your plans, rearrange your schedule, and even delete a couple of events.

Ah, but it's worth it.

After all, that's what best friends are for.

2

Playing It by the Book

They were just an average couple.

Oh, he probably would have been the quarterback on the football team, but football had not been invented. We're sure he would have been the corporate executive type since he showed real management skills, but he lived a good number of years before corporations. He certainly would have lived in the big house on the hill and driven an expensive car, but no one had ever thought of building houses, and gasoline was still in the bones of prehistoric animals.

She was the most gorgeous woman on the face of the earth. The historical record is clear on that point. She was thoughtful, deliberate, decisive. She would have been able to sort her way through to success even in our confusing times. We're positive she would have had a well-prepared things-to-do list except for the fact that pencils, paper, and writing had not been invented.

They were just an average couple.

Adam and Eve.

Average?

They were certainly the typical, normal couple of their day. They were the *only* couple of their day. Of course that had some advantages and some disadvantages.

How much time did Eve spend combing her hair? Certainly she never had it up in rollers on a Saturday night, since no one but the old man would see it on Sunday morning.

Think of the time saved by not having to worry about what to wear! There were no neighbors to keep up with, no bill collectors at the door, no telemarketing pitchmen on the phone, no kids to pick up after piano lessons, and no washing machines to break down.

How about Adam? What would it be like not to have to worry about house payments or where the next meal was coming from? There was no boss at work who was always on his case. No freeway traffic to hassle through. No grass to mow, weeds to pull, or garbage to take out!

With all of that going for them, we would expect Adam and Eve to be the best of friends. After all, what other choice did they have?

Chapters 2 and 3 of Genesis give us the picture of our ancient ancestors. In that account maybe there is a glimpse of friendship. Certainly Adam is quick to compliment. The minute he first saw Eve he said, "This is now bone of my bones, and flesh of my flesh" (Genesis 2:23). (Loosely paraphrased, "Wow! This is more like it!") We know that he believed in giving Eve some personal freedom, because she was confronted by the serpent directly (Genesis 3:1).

Eve was a decisive gal: "When the woman saw that the tree was good for food, and that it was a delight to the eyes, and that the tree was desirable to make one wise, she took from its fruit and ate" (Genesis 3:6).

And they did things together: "And she gave also to her husband with her, and he ate" (Genesis 3:6).

But there were certainly some elements of friendship missing from that garden scene. The two most notable: communication and spiritual discernment.

We keep wondering, if they were really such close friends—as we would expect the only two folks on earth to be—why weren't there long hours of discussion and debate about the forbidden fruit before such a temptation conquered them? We would have liked to hear Eve say, "Hey, big boy, come over here and listen to this snake. He sounds mighty convincing. What's your opinion?"

Second, more important than anything else, neither demonstrated a strong desire to be obedient to the Lord. Remember, the Lord didn't give them many instructions. Their list of "don'ts" was quite small: "But from the tree which is in the middle of the garden, God has said, 'You shall not eat from it or touch it, lest you die' " (Genesis 3:3).

God's rule for relationships was pretty simple. Adam and Eve didn't need it in writing—there was just one thing to remember: Don't even think of touching the fruit of that one tree.

So they disregarded God's clear word and brought upon them-selves all the trials and tribulations that couples have struggled with ever since—from childbirth to farming rough land—as is recorded in Genesis 3:14-19.

We sometimes despair at what they did. We say, "They had so little to comply with; how could they fail to obey?"

Yet the same statement could apply to many couples today. God's Word is more exhaustive and revealing in our day. A few more pages have been added to the text, yet the instruction is just as clear. Un-fortunately, we hold onto the ancestral trait of disregarding His Word.

Thus, square one for Adam and Eve, and for every couple since, is to find out what God has to say about husband and wife relationships and to pledge to be obedient to what we find.

It's a risky business. What if we find something we don't like? What if?

ORDERING THE HOME FOR MAXIMUM FRIENDSHIP

The husband and wife can do things that will maximize friendship in their marriage.

HUSBANDS

Five steps will help the husband build friendship into his marriage.

Stubbornly hold onto your wife. Look at Genesis 2:24 one more time. "For this cause a man shall leave his father and his mother, and shall cleave to his wife; and the two shall become one flesh."

What does that tell husbands to do? Cleave? What does that mean? It means to hold on to her and not let go. It means to touch and snuggle; to make her the focus of your thought. It means con-stantly to make her feel well-loved.

Before marriage, that is usually easy to do. Big, strong, cool, macho men have been known to do some amazingly silly things just to prove their love to a lady. But after the wedding service, he has the idea that she will know how much she is loved, even if he doesn't hold on as tightly. That's just not true.

Cleaving to her means you are continually finding new ways to show that love. Even when distance forces you apart, you can still cleave to her.

For two summers in a row Janet spent six weeks in northern Idaho while I continued the church ministry in southern California. The first year I came upon a way to show her I was still cleaving.

I determined to write her a letter.

Every day.

No matter what.

Whether I was traveling and speaking, at home on my day off, or down at the church flooded with busywork, Janet received an 8 1/2 by 11 inch, single spaced, full-page, typed letter every day. She couldn't go to the mailbox without discovering that I was indeed still holding on to her.

Sacrificially love your wife. It's right there in Ephesians 5:25: "Husbands, love your wives, just as Christ also loved the church and gave Himself up for her."

Now that puts real weight behind the word *love*. Some men "love" pickup trucks, horses that buck, and dogs that bark—but that has nothing to do with the kind of love mentioned here.

Jesus loved the church enough to hold back His full deity temporarily (Philippians 2:6-8), come to earth in human form (John 1:14), and die a torturous death on a cross for your sins and mine (I Corinthians 15:3). He did all of that with full knowledge of exactly who we really are. "But God demonstrates His own love toward us, in that while we were yet sinners, Christ died for us" (Romans 5:8).

That is exactly the kind of love God expects every husband to show his wife. Nothing less will suffice. Sacrificial love means a willingness to give something up to show your love. It means a willingness to give everything up to demonstrate your love.

Chuck loves Patty very much. Why, he gave her a dozen red roses and took her out to dinner at a lovely restaurant last Tuesday night.

Of course, her birthday was Monday . . . but the Chargers were playing the Seahawks on television, and there was no way he could miss that game.

Big deal.

Nothing less than sacrificial love will do.

Wisely lead your wife. Return to Ephesians 5; this time look at verse 23. "For the husband is the head of the wife, as Christ also is the head of the church."

Oh, how folks love to twist a verse like that to justify their own behavior. Yes, the husband is to be the biblical leader. But what kind of leader is he to be?

A petty tyrant?

A vengeful dictator?

A permissive wimp?

No.

A wise leader . . . just as Christ is the leader of His body, the church.

Wisdom is knowing the right goal to aim for and knowing the best way to achieve that goal. It takes biblical goals *and* biblical means to offer genuine leadership.

Providing for your family's material and educational needs is certainly a wise goal for which to aim. Spending the savings account on state lottery tickets is not a wise method of achieving that goal.

Lovingly nurture your wife in spiritual matters. Continuing in Ephesians 5, Paul says in verses 28 and 29, "He who loves his own wife loves himself; for no one ever hated his own flesh, but nourishes and cherishes it, just as Christ also does the church."

To nourish means to strengthen and to build up. To cherish means to hold in high value. Jesus constantly strengthens the church because it places such a high value on Him. So also must husbands physically, mentally, socially, economically, and spiritually build up their wives.

Now building her up does not mean to flatter her. Mere flattery —that is, praising qualities that she has no control over—is condescending. It is used only when you want selfishly to get something for yourself. Most wives see through such motives with amazing clarity.

Building her up means helping her develop all the gifts and talents and abilities that God has given her. It means helping her grow in knowledge of the Lord.

It does not nourish any wife's spirit to put obstacles in the way of her regular daily devotions, weekly Bible studies, or attendance at worship. It does not nourish her much to send her off to church to be the family's spiritual representative while you stay at home. It does not show much cherishing when you demand Sunday dinner at 12:00 noon.

Most husbands have no idea what they could do to help strengthen their wives' spiritual lives. Most husbands have never asked their wives for their suggestions.

Faithfully live with your wife. It was Jesus who said, "What therefore God has joined together, let no man separate" (Matthew 19:6). The question of divorce had come up, and some Pharisees were quizzing Jesus to get His opinion on the matter. They wanted to talk about divorce. Jesus wanted to talk about faithfulness. They wanted to know how to get out of marriage. Jesus reminded them to stick it out in marriage.

It is obvious that if you abandon a marriage relationship, you have destroyed the friendship as well. But it must also be noted that any marriage that fails to have daily faithfulness as the cornerstone will never build a strong friendship, no matter how many years folks might live together as husband and wife.

Harrison and Matty are neighbors down the street. In the ten years we've known them, we have never seen them angry with each other.

"Don't you two ever fight? You know, get mad at each other?" we questioned.

"Oh, sure," Harrison laughed. "We certainly have our fair share of disagreements."

"Then why doesn't it ever show?"

"Well, we usually get things solved rather quickly," Matty added.

"You see," Harrison explained, "We're in it for the long run. The question is not whether we will live a long life together. We've already decided that. The only question is, How are we going to live that long life? A lifetime of forgiveness seems a lot more pleasant than a lifetime of bitterness."

Being faithful means you always remember that you are in it for the long run.

WIVES

Four steps will help the wife build friendship into her marriage.

Be your husband's helper. Take one last trip to Genesis 2:18: "Then the Lord God said, 'It is not good for the man to be alone; I will make him a helper suitable for him.' "

The verse does not say that a wife is to be a slave or a servant. It does not say that a wife must do half of the physical labor (for some gals that would decrease the work load).

It does say that she is to be a helper. A friend to that lonely man. Look again . . . the verse mentions a lonely man who needs someone to walk alongside him in life. That's what a helper is all about.

Last summer we decided to put up lots of new wallpaper at our house. It was Steve's job to clean the walls, cut and soak the paper, balance on the chair, get the paper stuck to the walls, roll out the air bubbles, brush and sponge down the paper, make sure it was properly aligned with the previous section, and keep the excess paste from dripping on the carpet.

It was Janet's job to pick out the paper at the store, and sit on a stool and watch as Steve hung the paper. Not much help, you say? In that specific job, in our particular home, that is exactly the kind of help that was needed. When Steve gets to flying through a room with wallpaper, he needs someone to talk to—and no one in his way. "A helper suitable for him."

Accept your husband's leadership. Let's go back to the passage from Ephesians 5, this time looking at verses 22 and 24: "Wives, be subject to your own husbands, as to the Lord." "But as the church is subject to Christ; so also the wives ought to be to their husbands in everything."

At some point in the past forty years the expression "be subject to" has taken on negative connotations. The expression actually means to voluntarily surrender some of your own rights to the leadership of another. That is not involuntary slavery. It does not happen automatically. You must choose to accept your husband's leadership.

Notice what a positive view of subjection the Bible presents. In Luke 2:51 we are told that twelve-year-old Jesus was subject to His parents. Then in Romans 13:1 we are commanded to be subject to our government. Finally, in 1 Peter 5:5 we are reminded to be subject to the leaders of the church. In each case submissiveness is not a matter of losing what is rightfully ours; rather it is a voluntary acceptance of the order of relationships in which God has placed us.

Accepting a husband's leadership does not mean abandoning the role of confidant and counselor. He very much needs your wisdom. When that wisdom comes with faithful support, you'll find that his leadership decisions actually improve.

Respect your husband. The closing words to wives in Ephesians 5 state, "Let the wife see to it that she respect her husband" (v. 33).

To respect means to show honor and esteem for another. It is interesting that Paul singles out this one virtue for his concluding remarks to wives. Perhaps it is because it is too often missing. Respect for your husband is to be demonstrated in private, in front of the children, and in the presence of the general public.

You are not called to honor sinful, unbiblical behavior, or to hold it in high esteem. However, most of the lack of respect we see is not due to dismay over lapses. It is due to dismay over things that are not in themselves dishonorable. Some wives seem to have no problem putting down the vocation or pay scale of their husbands. Many seem to parade their husband's weaknesses in order to extol their own patience and virtue. The Ephesians passage prohibits such displays.

Learn to love your husband. In Titus 2:4 it is said that one of the roles of older women is to "encourage the young women to love their husbands."

Is this something that women need encouragement in? Obviously, or Paul's command is superfluous. More will be said in a later chapter about ways of expressing that love. The point here is this: the marriage vow is a formal affirmation that you love your husband in the present and promise to learn to love him even better as the years go by. In the total spectrum of things, you probably knew little about yourself at the time of your marriage, let alone knowing much about the true nature of your husband. That's why there was plenty left to learn. Even after years of marriage you will be just beginning to understand the complexities of his personality. Knowing him as well as you do now, but continuing to express your love in the same way you did five or ten or twenty years ago probably isn't sufficient.

A couple of times a year Janet packs my dufflebag, tosses me my old jean jacket and a sleeping bag, and tells me to get lost. Now it's not because she wants to get rid of me but because she loves me. After twenty-five years of marriage, she knows she can't get the wilderness blood out of a wilderness man. I thrive on long days in mountains and prairies without a person in sight. I spend a few days in the Arizona desert, the Rocky Mountains, or the canyons of Idaho and come back home refreshed. But it took a good number of years for Janet to learn to love me that much. During those first years, my departure would have caused her feelings of rejection. You have to keep learning to love.

While we didn't cover all the texts in this chapter, the picture is clear. God has a specific opinion about how we should establish the marriage relationship. Any serious desire to strengthen that relationship must begin by acknowledging His guidance. To try to build a satisfying, lasting, growing friendship in marriage without studying and obeying God's Word is as foolish as Adam and Eve's ignoring the one rule they were given. If we are at all serious in our quest to be our mate's best friend, we will certainly want to play it by the Book.

THE VALUE OF THE BIBLE'S TEACHING ON FRIENDSHIP

Just how does all this teaching from the Bible help friendships?

It eliminates competition. By defining what a husband should do and what a wife should do, the Bible keeps us from competing for the same position. If we are both striving to find acceptance in the mothering role, for instance, someone is going to be a loser. With the biblical roles in balance, both husband and wife will win.

It brings in a mutually accepted arbitrator. With the Bible as the final authority, the "my way" versus "your way" battle can be eliminated.

Instead, a couple can work together in order to discover His way. Too many marriages develop into a game of one-upmanship. Every time he gets her to do it "his way" he thinks he proves his superiority. The Bible, as an inerrant guide, eliminates such pettiness.

It allows freedom from the nonbiblical roles of society. Becoming free from the nonbiblical roles promoted by the society around us gives us the opportunity to develop into all that we are meant to be. The pressures and role models of society are fickle and arbitrary. If we don't read the latest ladies' magazine or watch this week's soap opera on television or keep up with the newest pop psychology book, we're afraid of being out of style and out of date.

Chris and Marlene are the ideal couple. She's an ex-cheerleader and former student body president and is currently a marine biologist. Chris graduated from the Air Force academy, served his time, and now works as an executive for a airplane manufacturing company. Their wedding last spring was lovely. All the little girls in church announced that they wanted to find a husband like Chris and have a wedding just like Marlene's.

Now it didn't surprise me all that much that the two of them came in for some counseling about six months after their wedding. There was no big problem, just some minor things that didn't seem quite right.

"It's not exactly like I thought it would be," Marlene announced.

"Yeah," Chris added, "are we doing something wrong?"

I assured them it was quite normal.

What Marlene and Chris now face is the long, joyful process of learning to be each other's best friend.

3

Remember, It's Just the Three of You

She was never elected president of the Women's Association. Nor was she ever the outreach chairman for the local garden club. It is certain that she never got a life achievement award from the P.T.A.

All such prestigious accomplishments take time to achieve. They are most often given to one who has proved over the years to be a faithful, constant worker for the benefit of the organization and community.

Now it's not that she didn't want those things. It was . . . well, you know . . . her husband. He was one of those . . . how can we say it? . . . traveling men. He just wouldn't ever settle down. Poor thing. Just about the time her fruit trees started producing, he would up and move the family to . . . who knows where.

Frankly, she should have put her foot down. From Ur of the Chaldeans to Haran, down across the desert, into the Jordan Valley, south of the Dead Sea, up into the mountains, through the Negev into Egypt, back to Canaan . . . can you imagine dragging your furniture through all that?

Fortunately, at first she didn't have children to worry about. All the same, she should have looked him in the eye and said, "Abraham, we're not moving again!"

Though Sarah was culturally adapted to the nomadic lifestyle, the point remains: she was extremely loyal to Abraham. There is hardly a scene where she is not by his side.

Loyalty is a decisive, voluntary act. If it is forced by another, it ceases to be loyalty. It becomes slavery. Loyalty is the pledge of allegiance to another person. It's saying, "Whatever happens, I'm on your side."

Visalia. Ivanhoe. Sacramento. Coalinga. Pasadena. Los Angeles. Woodlake. Fillmore. Winchester. What do these places have in common? We've lived in every one of them. Eighteen moves in twenty-five years of marriage. And what are we talking about now? Perhaps another move. Through it all, Janet has stuck it out. It's part of the picture of loyalty.

THE LOOK OF LOYALTY

LOYALTY MEANS GOING OFF INTO THE UNKNOWN

Abraham's call in Genesis 12:1-4 is rather ambiguous. The Lord told him that he was to go "to the land which I will show you." Can you imagine the dialogue around the supper table that night?

"Well, pack our things up. We're leaving in the morning."

"Oh, are we taking a little vacation, dear?"

"No, we're moving."

"Moving? Where?"

"I don't know."

"You don't know?"

"I don't know . . . exactly. He didn't say."

"Who didn't say?"

"God."

"God told us to move, but He didn't say where?"

"Right."

"Well, how long will we be traveling? Is the journey long?"

"He didn't say."

"Will it be hot or cold?"

"He didn't say."

"Will we ever come back here?"

"He didn't say."

"What did He say!"

"Just to pack up, and leave, and follow His leading, and everything will turn out fine . . . eventually."

"You expect me to accept that story?"

"Yep."

And she did, of course. Loyal Sarah stuck by her man, wherever he was headed.

It was one week before the wedding and all the plans had been made. There was nothing left to do but wait and worry about caterers, tuxedo rentals, and bouquets. Finally, the bride and groom could stop to catch their breath before the big event. We were surprised when Margaret called us at about nine o'clock on Saturday night.

"Bruce just brought over a pre-nuptial contract a mile long—and the wedding's off," she cried.

Three hours later, after counseling with each separately and both together, the wedding was back on again.

With a little free time on his hands while Margaret was made last minute plans, Bruce had had some second thoughts about the idea of marriage. Oh, he knew that he loved Margaret. He knew also that they both loved the Lord. But marriage was such a big unknown all of a sudden. What if things didn't turn out the way they planned?

What if Margaret changed her mind about his going to graduate school?

What if she suddenly made him get rid of his country and western tapes?

What if she didn't want to wait five years to have children?

What if she didn't want their future son to go to U.C.L.A.?

She wouldn't move back to Mississippi with the kids if he got munched on the job, would she?

If they split up, who would get the '56 Corvette? And the antique pool table?

On and on the questions rolled in Bruce's mind. The only solution was to spell out all the contingencies in a pre-nuptial contract.

So he thought.

Margaret saw it differently. She saw a lack of commitment, loyalty, and trust. Fortunately, it didn't take long for Bruce to see it that way also. He was just afraid of the unknown. We all are.

Loyalty in marriage means we trudge off into occupations, neighborhoods, ministries, ideas, hobbies, projects, organizations, and parenthood not knowing where it will all lead; but knowing that whatever happens, the two of us will face them one by one, together.

Loyalty might mean she comes home and announces, "I signed us up for a Couples Conference at the lake." And you trudge off hand in hand.

Loyalty might mean he comes home and announces, "I bought us a grocery store in Yellowknife, Northwest Territories." And you trudge north hand in hand.

LOYALTY MEANS STICKING TOGETHER THROUGH FOOLISH ACTIONS

For a man called "Father of our faith," it was a foolish action. Perhaps it showed some of the struggle Abraham was having in trusting God—the same kind of struggle we are all going through.

He and Sarah had left home and wandered through the land called Canaan. Somewhere in that region, God would show them their destination. But in the meantime, famine struck.

The pressure and guilt must have weighed heavily upon Abraham. "I took her away from home, pulled her away from her relatives, marched her through the wilderness. Now we've reached this land and we still do not possess any for ourselves. On top of that, we have the famine. What a great husband I turned out to be."

Abraham decided that they had better go to Egypt where food and supplies could be found more easily (Genesis 12:10-20). His doubts and fears grew into near paranoia. Sarah was a beautiful woman. What if some jealous Egyptian killed him to get Sarah for his own wife?

So he devised a great little plan whereby Sarah would pretend to be his sister. Not only would he be safe that way, Abraham surmised, but he might receive a few gifts and favors for being the brother of such a beautiful woman.

It was a dumb idea. It showed how little he was trusting God to keep His promises. It demonstrated a higher regard for personal gain and reward than for integrity and honesty. And it certainly put Sarah in a difficult and potentially dangerous situation.

Fortunately, God was not going to let Abraham and Sarah mess up His plan for their lives. It was His miraculous intervention that saved the day.

Through it all, Sarah demonstrated amazing loyalty. It's the kind of thing a best friend would do.

The Goldmine produced meals, not metal. It was, in the late seventies, the best place to eat in town. Kenneth and Sandi spent almost every waking hour seeing that their restaurant operated smoothly. There are rewards for hard work. They owned a two-story house on the hill with one of the largest swimming pools in town. Kenneth drove a German sports car, and Sandi liked her furs and diamonds. They were good, solid citizens, faithful church attenders, and cautious in their investments.

It surprised all of us when they announced one Sunday evening that they were going to sell the restaurant and their house to do mission work in West Africa. Some folks didn't think they were the type. Others advised caution and moderation. "Don't go overboard on this too quickly," they advised.

By the end of summer, Kenneth and Sandi had sold all their belongings and headed overseas. They wrote to us often. And they faced one disaster after another.

They had sent some funds ahead of them to secure housing and office space for a bookstore, but when they arrived they discovered that someone had absconded with all the funds. An auto accident sent Sandi to the hospital with a broken leg, and complications meant a flight to London to a specialist. Their health insurance did not cover any bills they incurred in that particular country, because there was civil war going on in the south.

Their cross-cultural training had been limited, and Kenneth proceeded to alienate most of the folks they were supposed to be reaching by insisting that meals be cooked according to modern American restaurant standards.

During the second year, their bookstore was robbed four times, and Kenneth got sick with a respiratory disease none of the doctors could diagnose. For a while he could survive only with a rare and expensive tank of oxygen close by.

Three years, two months, and eleven days after they left for the mission field, Kenneth and Sandi returned home. Only this time there was no thriving business, no house on the hill, no fur coats, no German car, and no diamonds. They live in a little apartment on the highway behind the supermarket. Sandi is the office manager at an insurance company, and Kenneth isn't strong enough to go back to work yet. Neither needs to be told that they jumped into that ministry unprepared.

Recently after a long day at work, Sandi sat in an office with several others from the church making plans for an upcoming event. "Well, if we still had the swimming pool . . ." then she caught herself and sighed. A tear came to her eye, and a big, warm smile rearranged the wrinkles on her face. "No regrets," she added. "I wouldn't have missed it for the world."

Loyalty means sticking with each other, no matter what.

LOYALTY MEANS GROWING OLD TOGETHER

We are never told just how old Abraham and Sarah were when they got married. We can only guess. If Abraham was thirty and Sarah twenty, then they would have been married forty-five years before they left Haran for the promised land. In addition, they would have been husband and wife for seventy years before their son, Isaac, was born. And their life together wasn't over. After the birth of Isaac, they spent thirty-seven more years together. That's almost forty thousand days of waking up with the same person next to you.

Can you imagine the changes that took place in their looks after 107 years together? Could they even remember when the hair was not grey, or the bones not weak, or the voice not halting and hoarse?

Genesis 23 records the death of Sarah: "And Sarah died in Kiriath-arba (that is, Hebron) in the land of Canaan; and Abraham went in to mourn for Sarah and to weep for her." Of course he wept. His most loyal friend of over a hundred years was gone.

The beautiful handmade fishing rod exuded a skill in craftmanship that few still possess. It was the envy of anyone who traveled north into the Sierras to fish with Herb. Some men seem born with a rod in their hand. Herb was one of those guys. He and Thelma traveled the West, fishing in every lake and stream imaginable. But there was no thrill greater for Herb than to take his handmade rod and hike into a little, high country stream and pull out a couple of big, fat trout.

That's what made his donation of that special rod to the community auction so surprising. "What about all those big ones that are still up there begging to be caught?" we teased.

"One of you young boys will have to snag them, if you can," Herb replied. "I won't be going back to the high country anymore."

"No more fishing?" we gasped.

"Well, the doc said Thelma's heart is getting so bad she shouldn't go up to those high elevations. So I figure now's a good time to retire. You know, we aren't kids anymore."

It was just the next step in growing old together. That's what loyalty is all about.

LOYALTY MEANS ACCEPTING THE LORD'S LEADING TOGETHER

We have no idea how much Abraham told Sarah. Over the years God had spoken to him on numerous occasions. She knew he was a good man. He tried to follow the Lord. Oh sure, there had been some failures. Sometimes they had done some dumb things, but they were learning to trust God to do what He said He would do.

The Lord had promised a son, and in His timing a son was born. They could now relax and enjoy their declining years with this child of the promise. Then in Genesis 22 we read of God's speaking to Abraham once more. Perhaps it was the final time the Lord spoke to him in such an audible manner. This time the instruction was to take Isaac to a specific mountain and offer him up as a burnt offering to the Lord. It was a shocking request.

How did Abraham tell Sarah? Perhaps he didn't. Perhaps he couldn't. But perhaps after that many years of married friendship, he indeed let her know what was happening. We do know that she didn't complain. We know that this woman who had wandered wilderness and city with Abraham had learned to trust his decisions. Remember, it was Sarah (in Genesis 16:3) who instigated the events that led to the birth of Ishmael by Hagar her servant. But now, when there was a possibility of losing her son of the promise, Sarah did not protest Abraham's actions. Peter says that "Sarah obeyed Abraham, calling him lord" (1 Peter 3:6). She had learned to trust what God was doing in her husband's life.

We two Blys came to Christ at nearly the same time. During most of those first months we encouraged each other in our spiritual growth. Steve was a farmer, and Janet a busy mother and homemaker.

The future of our lives included the Lord—as well as plowing fields, pruning trees, and harvesting crops.

"You want to what?" Janet asked.

"I think the Lord wants me to be a preacher," Steve announced.

"Don't you need some training?"

"Oh sure, I'll need two more years of college and at least three years of seminary."

"Five years? How about me and the kids?" she worried.

"The Lord will take care of our needs," Steve added.

"But you don't know how to preach. I mean, you don't even like to speak to crowds," she added.

"The truth is, I'm scared spitless to be in front of people," Steve continued, "but I believe that's what God wants me to do."

So Janet went to work, Steve went to school, and the kids learned what it was like to grow up poor.

It was what God wanted to do in Steve's life . . . and Janet encouraged him through every tough moment of it.

That's what loyalty in marriage is all about.

How Does Building Loyalty Increase Friendship in Marriage?

LOYALTY DESTROYS LONELINESS

Every act of loyalty from a mate reinforces the knowledge that "I am not alone." No longer are there thoughts of his plans versus her plans, his career versus her career, his money versus her money. It is now "our plans," "our career," and "our money."

Loyalty also means there will always be someone to talk to.

LOYALTY DEMONSTRATES ONENESS

The Bible does not say that marriage is merely a business partnership. You and your mate are not individual members of a "team." Genesis 2:24 states clearly that you become one. Loyalty in marriage is the element which shows that you understand that calling.

LOYALTY PROVIDES A BACKDROP FOR EXPRESSING YOUR DREAMS

It means there is always someone to rush home to and breathlessly exclaim, "Honey, I've got a great idea!" When you have loyalty in marriage, you know that you are always included in his or her plans. There is always someone who is on your side ready to listen, encourage, and advise.

LOYALTY PROPELS PROBLEMS TO A SPEEDY SOLUTION

Too often we try to solve problems by ignoring them or by moving away from them. But you can't ignore a loyal mate. You can't even move out of the room. You are blessed (or stuck, depending on your mood at the moment) with an intimate relationship with this person until death. Since there is no escape, it is mandatory that we solve differences quickly and resolve irritations daily.

LOYALTY GIVES YOU AN IDENTITY BEYOND YOUR OWN LIMITATIONS

There are times, of course, when we miss the independence of singleness. But the strengths our companion brings to the partnership enhance our own usefulness. Though most of us are quite willing to accept the laurels of success on our own, we appreciate being able to share the defeats and failures. Loyalty in marriage means you will always be in it together. Success and failure are always viewed as a team effort.

Loyalty, like many qualities in marriage, finds its deepest expression in God's loyalty to us.

How grateful we should be that our mates are spared from seeing every thought in our minds. Most times we filter out the worst before we ever speak a word. But the Lord always knows the worst. He sees all we have done, are doing, and will do. He knows what we have thought, are thinking, and will think in the future.

In spite of all that, He sent His Son to die for us. "But God demonstrates His own love toward us, in that while we were yet sinners, Christ died for us" (Romans 5:8).

He promises to forgive us always: "If we confess our sins, He is faithful and righteous to forgive us our sins and to cleanse us from all unrighteousness" (1 John 1:9).

And He will, one day, come back and take us home with Him: "And if I go and prepare a place for you, I will come again and receive you to Myself; that where I am, there you may be also" (John 14:3).

God loves us, forgives us, and won't ever give up on us. Now that is loyalty!

He would like some loyalty in return, of course. In Hosea 6:6, He states clearly, "For I delight in loyalty rather than sacrifice." But how can forgiven man, struggling to throw off a sinful nature, learn to be loyal to a holy, perfect, unseen God? We do so by demonstrating wholehearted loyalty to our God-given mate.

There is an interlocking of relationships here. You are only as loyal to your mate as you are to the Lord. And you are only as loyal to the Lord as you are to your mate. Marriage is a three-way friendship. So working at increasing loyalty will not only strengthen your marital friendship but will deepen your life with the Lord as well.

A SELF-CHECK TEST TO DISCOVER WEAKNESS IN MARITAL LOYALTY

1. When your mate says, "Hey, Babe, I read something in a magazine today that is going to change our life!" you
   a. shout, "Oh no, not another hair-brained scheme!"
   b. turn up the volume on the television.
   c. head for the refrigerator for something to eat.
   d. immediately listen to the whole proposal.
2. When your mate's invention for drying out the kids' tennis shoes in the microwave explodes, you tell the firemen,
   a. "I said over and over it wouldn't work."
   b. "Please don't ask questions. I don't want to talk about it."
   c. "I'm the only one in this family with any brains."
   d. "Well, we certainly learned our lesson on this one."
3. When your mate trips on a radish at the salad bar and untosses a bowl full of greens and dressing into the lap of a large lady in a white pantsuit, you
   a. decide that it's a good time for you to take a potty break.
   b. stare out the window at the parking lot, pretending that you didn't see a thing.

c. burst out laughing, pointing out the incident to others in the restaurant who might have missed it.

d. you offer your sincere apology to the lady in white and quickly help your mate clean up and regain some composure.

4. When your mate's emergency hospital bill eats up all the savings for that special anniversary trip, you say,

a. "If only you had waited to get sick until after June eighth!"

b. "I just knew this trip was too good to be true."

c. "Well, at least we still have enough money for one of us to go to Hawaii."

d. "You know, this might be a good year to go camping after all."

A Loyalty-Strengthening Project

If you answered anything but *d* to the questions above, you might want to consider a loyalty-strengthening project or two.

- Make "It's You and Me" cards. Both the husband and the wife should take a stack of 3" x 5" cards and handwrite on each, "I'm on your side! How can I help?" Keep your supplies handy . . . in the car, in the kitchen, in your pocket. Whenever you notice your mate is really up against it . . . with the boss, with the kids, with the clerk at the store, with his own imperfections . . . smile, and hand him (or her) a card. It's what a loyal friend does.

- Disregard your sacred "Things to Do List." Your mate is facing a tough situation—maybe an important decision, a hostile relationship, or an anxiety-producing performance. Toss away your calendar, cancel appointments, ditch the kids, and be there. Sit up front in the audience, hold your spouse's hand in the waiting room, or attend the parent-teacher conference together.

- Let the wrinkles remind you to praise. Every sign of aging you spot in your mate has been thoroughly examined and anguished over a thousand times before you even notice it. Never mention it to your mate. Just let the creases around the eyes or the bulge you see at the mid-section remind you of all the years you two

have put in together, and how great it is to grow old with someone who loves you.

Just you, your mate, and God.
It's called loyalty.
Oh, you might be able to have a marriage without much of it.
But who wants to?

4

You'll Know Who Loves Ya, Baby

He: How beautiful you are, my darling, how beautiful you are! Your eyes are like doves.

She: How handsome you are, my beloved, and so pleasant! Indeed, our couch is luxuriant! I am the rose of Sharon, the lily of the valleys.

He: Your hair is like a flock of goats that have descended from Mount Gilead. Your teeth are like a flock of newly shorn ewes which have come up from their washing, all of which bear twins, and not one of them has lost her young. Your lips are like a scarlet thread, and your mouth is lovely. Your temples are like a slice of a pomegranate behind your veil. Your neck is like the tower of David built with rows of stones, on which are hung a thousand shields, all the round shields of the mighty men. Your two breasts are like two fawns, twins of a gazelle which feed among the lilies. You are altogether beautiful, my darling, and there is no blemish in you.

She: My beloved is dazzling and ruddy, outstanding among ten thousand. His head is like gold, pure gold; his locks are like clusters of dates, and black as a raven. His eyes are like doves, beside streams of water, bathed in milk and reposed in their setting. His cheeks are like a bed of balsam, banks of sweet-scented herbs; his lips are lilies, dripping with liquid myrrh. His hands are rods of gold set with beryl; his abdomen is

carved ivory inlaid with sapphires. His legs are pillars of ala-
baster set on pedestals of pure gold; His appearance is like
Lebanon, choice as the cedars. His mouth is full of sweetness.
And he is wholly desirable. This is my beloved and this is my
friend, O daughters of Jerusalem.

Pure mush.

OK, the language is a tad archaic, but it is the type of thing high
school freshmen still write on the backs of their algebra assignments.
It's how you describe your fiancée to your old neighborhood playmate
you haven't seen in twelve years. It's the diary entry of a bride-to-be
or a love letter home from a soldier stationed overseas.

"He" is King Solomon (c. 965 B.C.), and "she" is a Shulammite
woman who is about to become his bride. The text comes straight
out of the Bible—Song of Solomon 1:15-2:1; 4:1-5,7; 5:10-16.

The text, especially the graphic descriptions in it of the sexual attraction the couple feels for one another, has embarrassed many of us
for years. It shouldn't. Married love includes physical attraction. The
spoken or written word is one way to express that love to your mate.
Maybe what intimidates us most about the text of Song of Solomon
is how impoverished our own descriptions of each other tend to be.
When was the last time a husband wrote, "Your belly is like a heap of
wheat fenced about with lilies" (Song of Solomon 7:2)? Or how long
has it been since you heard a wife say, "Like an apple tree among the
trees of the forest, so is my beloved among the young men. In his
shade I took great delight and sat down. And his fruit was sweet to
my taste" (Song of Solomon 2:3)?

Surely only the very young or newlyweds employ such terms as
these. If that's true, it's a shame. If we no longer look for, plot out, or
devise our own unique creative terms of affection, we impoverish our
marriage and weaken our friendship.

The Shulammite bride summed up her feelings for her groom:
"This is my beloved and this is my friend, O daughters of Jerusalem"
(Song of Solomon 5:16).

Beloved and friend.

That's what marriage is all about. We are to be friends and lovers.
To strengthen our love for each other is to strengthen our friendship.

THREE ASPECTS OF LOVE FOR YOUR MATE

There is a *physical* dimension of our love. In the presence of our mate we feel terrific. Our bodies feel vibrant, alive, and sexy. To touch them and to have them touch us is exciting.

A quick pat, hug, kiss, or caress can make a bad day good, and a good day thrilling!

There is also the *spiritual* depth to our love. The deepest expression of this spiritual depth is felt by two individuals who each have a vibrant relationship with Jesus Christ as Lord and Savior and together have committed themselves to following God's leading. But even nonbelievers have a spiritual dimension to their marriage, for God's decree, "They shall become one flesh" (Genesis 2:24), was for all people, for all times.

That spiritual union is designed by God. It's His wedding present to every married couple. Deep beneath the surface feelings and even beneath the consciousness of the mind is a spiritual bond that provides a foundation for our love.

There is also a *mental* assent to our love. This is the act of the will of the individual who says, "I choose to love you." Humans are created with the free will to direct their love. We are allowed to direct our love toward God or to withhold it from Him. We are allowed to direct our love toward a member of the opposite sex of our choosing. We must decide to love him or her.

LOVE THAT KEEPS GROWING

Friendship in marriage requires a love that doesn't stagnate but keeps growing.

We cannot add to the spiritual union of our marriage. That is the Lord's department. At the moment we consummated our marriage He granted us a spiritual union. We cannot increase that union (although we can develop the outward signs of it), but we can destroy it. "Consequently they are no longer two, but one flesh. What therefore God has joined together, let no man separate" (Matthew 19:6).

In addition, we cannot always predict how the physical dimension of our married love will develop. Oh, we may lose weight, try a new hair style, and buy some new clothes, but there is no guarantee that passion will increase.

Every married couple can remember the time. It was probably a Friday night. The wife arranged for the kids to stay at grandma's. The husband brought home a beautiful corsage. Mrs. put on her beautiful, tasteful (of course), but slightly revealing new gown. Mr. got out the good suit and the black tie and polished his shoes. You went to that new French restaurant on the hill and ordered the finest of everything. There were little smiles, laughs, and touches at that secluded corner table. You talked on and on past dinner, past coffee, past dessert. You tipped the waiter generously and laughed and giggled your way home to an empty house and a waiting bed. But the truth of the matter was, by the time you put out the cat, locked the doors, and brushed your teeth, neither of you was really interested in making love. That physical feeling can't always be programmed.

But remember the time husband came in from cleaning the garage? The kids had half the neighborhood in the living room and the Mrs. was in the closet hanging up clothes. Hubby was wearing those grubby old jeans that the wife kept trying to throw away. Besides that, it was Saturday, and he hadn't even shaved.

Of course, the wife wasn't exactly looking her best either. She had run a quick comb through her hair, looked in the mirror and exclaimed "Oh well, we won't be seeing anyone today anyway." She was wearing that old, dark dress that would have been too conservative for even a Puritan. Besides that, she still had soapy water on the back of her hands from loading the washing machine.

Nonetheless, when hubby brushed against her as he reached into the closet for a clean shirt, something electric passed between the two. She held onto his arm, and he embraced her waist. The next thing they knew, the closet door was shut, the light was turned out, and they were embracing.

Sometimes the physical feeling cannot be predicted. It would be disappointing to sit around waiting for our feelings to increase.

But we can do a lot to increase the mental aspect of our love commitment in marriage. It is at this point that love can grow and grow.

A couple which has a growing friendship will have a growing love relationship because they are choosing actions that demonstrate their love.

How do you say "I love you" to your mate?

Dr. Gary Chapman, the author of *Toward a Growing Marriage* and *Hope for the Separated* (both Chicago: Moody), says that there are five love languages, five different ways humans express love. Chapman challenges us to discover our mate's primary love langauge so that we can express our love in that language. The five love languages Dr. Chapmen mentions include words, gifts, actions, quality time, and physical touch.

We want to push just a bit beyond that. We have found that most mates need a variety of love expressions from time to time, and the five love languages are a starting point for expanding our expressions of love.

Discovering New Ways to Say "I Love You"

TRY USING WORDS

Obviously, every married person spends time telling his mate, "I love you." Right?

Wrong.

Some seem to be operating under the assumption that once they say "I do" at the altar, no further comment is needed. Others tend to limit the phrase to the moments immediately preceding a request. "I love you. Oh, can I have $60 to go shopping?" Or, "I love you. Why don't we go to bed and make love?"

Now we can all be a little more creative than that. Here are some other ways of verbally saying, "I love you."

When your mate least expects it . . . Call the bowling alley right in the middle of his league, get him on the phone and say, "I was just thinking about how much I love you." Or call her away from the P.T.A. board meeting to say, "I just wanted you to know I'm crazy about you." Think of what it will do for her when she reports to her friends on this "emergency" call.

In front of the relatives . . . You know, at the big Thanksgiving dinner when his folks are there, as well as all the aunts, uncles, and cousins. Grab your spouse by the waist, plant a long, soft kiss right on the lips, and say in a convincing tone, "Wow, I really love you!"

Write a mushy poem . . . You read about it at the first of this chapter. Be descriptive. Mention the things you really like about him or her. Slip it in a birthday card, or anniversary greeting. Sure, he might say, "Boy, you went a little overboard on this." But we guarantee that it will get tucked away in the sock drawer and read over and over again.

Try "first strike" for a whole week . . . Every time you see your mate after any type of separation make the first words on your lips, "I love you." When you two first wake up . . . "I love you." When he gets home from work . . . "I love you." When she returns from the grocery store . . . "I love you." When he returns from watching Junior's Little League game . . . "I love you." Strike first with verbal love.

For about two hours one Friday morning, a young man stood on the street corner of our little home town with a big sandwich board type sign. It read on front and back in hand-scrawled letters, "I love you, Rosie!"

The daily newspaper flashed his photo as a human interest story on the front page of the features section. It seems that Rosie is his wife and Friday was her birthday. It has become quite popular in our area to take out a display ad in the paper to wish someone a happy birthday. He had wanted to do that for his Rosie, but some extra medical expenses prevented him. So he figured he would get his greeting in the paper another way. He succeeded.

TRY NEW WAYS OF GIVING GIFTS

To many folks, an unaccounted for gift is a high expression of love. "Unaccounted for" means that no one expects you to give it. It means if you didn't do it, your mate would not feel slighted. Miss a birthday, anniversary, or Christmas and he will be crushed. Those are the expected gifts. You can really say "I love you" with the unexpected ones.

Send your love ahead of him . . . Whenever he has to go on a trip, order a special present to get there before him. You can have a bowl of fruit waiting at the hotel, a crazy balloon in the lobby of the national headquarters, or a present secretly tucked in the suitcase to be discovered when he first opens it.

Treat your mate to a "home shopping" spree . . . Send for a gift certificate to your mate's favorite mail order catalog. Then hand your mate the latest edition of the catalog and the gift certificate and say, "Go for it!" Then stay out of the way, and let him (or her) select the item(s) without one word of direction from you.

Give your mate a gift in public . . . Carry a present with you when you meet for lunch, and have your mate open it at the restaurant. Greet your mate at his place of employment with a present that can be opened in front of all his colleagues. Meet him at the airport or subway station or bus stop with a gift to be opened on the spot.

Celebrate an off-beat anniversary with a gift . . . Maybe the fifth anniversary of not having to change a dirty diaper. Or the twenty-fifth time you accidently set off the fire alarm. Or the first time in history your mate passed by a Mrs. Field's store without buying a chocolate chip cookie.

We had all gathered around on the set—the director, producer, cameramen, sound technicians, talk show host, and their special guests, the Blys—to pray before the program began. Just as the circle joined hands, in walked a person in a clown costume with a delivery of balloons and a small gum ball machine for one of the cameramen. His face turned bright red.

"Oh no, it's from Marcie, my wife! She did it again."

"Is it a special day?" we asked.

"No, that's just the way she is," he sheepishly mumbled. "She's always doing things like this."

Smart gal.

She's got a marriage that's growing in love.

TRY NEW ACTIONS FOR YOUR MATE'S BENEFIT

You can show love to your mate through acts of service. It is obviously a statement of love to spend three hours cooking a meal that takes twenty minutes to consume and two hours to clean up. It must be love to come home after a grueling day at work and paint the kitchen cabinets to match the new towels she bought. The very fact that he crawled out of bed at 5:00 A.M., fought his way through rush hour traffic, and hassled out another day at the office is in itself a great act of love.

Tackle your mate's most horrible job . . . Somewhere around the house is that chore he has labeled as "the lousiest thing I'm stuck with." It's probably one of those chores that you are completely thankful is his responsibility and not yours. Maybe it's scrubbing the toilets, cleaning the mold out of the shower, cleaning the garage, washing the pickup, hoeing the weeds out back, or whatever. Without consulting him, do it for him, unannounced and without fanfare. When he gasps "Why?" answer, "I just wanted you to know who loves you."

Pounce on your mate's next request . . . Every wife and husband has a "things to do list." They are those actions you want to see the other one accomplish. Often the wife's list is written down and the husband's merely in his head, but both have a list. The very next time your mate says, "Honey, I sure would appreciate it if sometime you could. . . ." drop everything and do it at that moment. He says, "Remember that strawberry custard you used to make when we first got married?" By evening he's eating one. She says, "I wish that garage door was fixed." Before supper that night the job is done.

Be a secret helper . . . Tackle a project for your spouse, but try to get it done without letting him or her even know you're doing it. Fellas, you get up early some morning and discover she didn't have time to get the dishes done the night before. Wash them without waking her. Then head off to work as usual. Gals, go outside when hubby is gone and scrub his barbecue until it shines; then slip it back into the garage and don't mention a word.

Be a volunteer assistant . . . Announce to your mate, "I have two hours on Saturday, what chore around the house can I help you get done?" Help her rearrange the living room furniture. Help him sort out his fishing tackle. You are the assistant, and you are ready for any assignment.

Our friend Connie went to visit her mother one Friday. When she got home about noon on Saturday, there was something different about the kitchen. As she buzzed around cooking dinner, she began to notice a few of the dishes and appliances were not quite in their normal place. Then it hit her.

"Shelf paper! It's all new shelf paper. You took everything out and put in new shelf paper!" she blurted at Ed.

"Hey, I had some time. No big deal," he replied.

"My friends are not going to believe this," she added. "I mean, I really got one of the good ones."

Connie's right.

INVEST MORE QUALITY TIME IN EACH OTHER

Quality time. It's an over-worked phrase. It means time that is spent on only one subject. It means you do not immerse yourself in your needlepoint while he tells you about the struggle he's having at work. It means you do not stare at football on television while she agonizes over what to do about Sissy's grades.

Schedule a regular appointment with your mate . . . Crazy? You already know what happens when you say, "We'll have to talk about that sometime." You never find the time, do you? So how about every Thursday night, 8:30–10:00 P.M.? No matter what happens, that is your time alone to talk in private. Of course you talk other times, but that gives you a guarantee of not being too busy for each other.

Instigate an open door policy . . . Let your mate know you are available to listen to him at any time, in any place. Let him know that it is all right to interrupt any action. He may call during a golf game or at the supermarket. She may interrupt Monday night football, and he may interrupt Tuesday afternoon soap opera. You will stop in the middle of sewing a dress or building the kitchen cabinets . . . if your mate needs your attention.

Volunteer to spend an evening doing something your mate really likes but never gets to do because you aren't the least bit interested . . . Hop into his pickup and go to the Merle Haggard concert with him. Rent a tux and take her to her favorite ballet.

Park the car in a quiet spot and watch the sun go down . . . Don't you have some memories about times before marriage when you parked the car and spent hours talking? Why did you choose the car? Because it was private and free from interruptions. Times haven't changed. You might still need the isolation of your auto to make the time really count.

We have a funny way of selecting restaurants. When we first got married all we cared about was finding a place we could afford . . . like the ninety-nine cent steak house specials before 5 P.M. on Monday nights. Then we moved into the gourmet era when we were looking for good, wholesome food with "character." Fresh fruit and vegetables and a salad with alfalfa sprouts were a must.

But now we forget about the price and aren't as picky about the food—what we want is a restaurant with comfortable, private booths, so we can sit for long hours and talk. Time with each other has taken priority over bargains and cuisine.

KEEP LEARNING HOW TO BE A BETTER LOVER

We express love by physical touch. This can be as relaxed as an arm around the waist or as intense as intercourse. One of the greatest mistakes in our present society is the assumption so many men and women make that they are experts in physical love.

When we get married, we don't need a general practitioner who has ample knowledge about the opposite sex. What we want and need is a specialist who is going to become an expert in making love to just one person. We are all amateurs in that regard, but we needn't stay that way.

Accept the fact that all expressions of physical affection do not have to lead to bed . . . If you've been a little lazy, rediscover the joy of a walk while holding hands . . . cuddling while watching television

. . . kissing on the beach at sunset . . . huddling up in the cold stands at the football game. None of these actions has to lead to sex. Take time to enjoy them without plotting where it will lead.

Sit down and ask each other—"How can I be a better lover for you?" Listen to your mate. His (or her) suggestions are not statements about your failure but rather about the desire for the excitement in physical love to keep growing. Maybe your mate will tell you something easy—like cut your fingernails closer. Maybe it will be something difficult—like slow down and take more time. But keep talking; let your mate know you intend to be the best lover on earth for him (or her).

Discuss just how much physical affection you are comfortable with in public . . . If you tend to be more physical in public, back down to a level that is best for your mate. If your mate is more physical in public, push yourself a little to try and meet his (or her) needs.

Absolutely refuse to mention to others any complaints you have regarding your mate's lovemaking ability . . . Wise cracks about frigid wives or slobbery husbands should not be told. If your child is learning to play the piano and you only talk about his mistakes when you are in public, your child will want to quit. Instead, of course, you always mention those things he is doing well in order to encourage him to do better. Why would we think learning to love another person is any different? Or any easier?

We've been married twenty-six years. That's almost 9,500 nights of crawling into bed with the same person. Thousands and thousands of hugs, snuggles, hand holding, good night kisses, and sexual encounters. We've been working at loving each better and better most of those years. What advice do we have? We have learned that during the first twenty years you are merely amateurs. You don't get really reach your prime until sometime between twenty and thirty years. So keep in there. Keep practicing, keep learning, keep growing in your expressions of physical love.

Friends are people who love you.

A good friend really expresses his love in a variety of ways.
A best friend can make you feel loved more than all others in the
whole world . . . combined.

5
Don't Ask Mom . . . Ask Dad!

Little Jake was a Mamma's boy.

His brother liked running through the fields and across the wilderness; Jake liked playing at home.

His brother would grab a stick, make a pretend bow and arrow, and stalk rabbits in a make-believe hunt. Jake liked helping his mother bake bread.

His brother was a bit reckless in making decisions—whatever would help him most at the moment usually determined his actions. Jake was shrewd and calculating. Every move was meant to lead him to achieve his goals in life.

His brother could fight his way out of most tight squeezes. Jake could talk his way out of nearly anything. Daddy loved his brother more. But that was all right—everyone knew that Mamma loved Jake best.

It says so right there in the Bible: "When the boys grew up, Esau became a skillful hunter, a man of the field; but Jacob was a peaceful man, living in tents. Now Isaac loved Esau, because he had a taste for game; but Rebekah loved Jacob" (Genesis 25:27-28).

The boys didn't get along too well. The day came when Jacob bribed the firstborn's birthright from Esau, and finally Jacob deceived old Isaac so that he could steal the firstborn's blessing. To say the boys had a few disagreements would be an understatement.

"So Esau bore a grudge against Jacob because of the blessing with which his father had blessed him; and Esau said to himself, 'The days of mourning for my father are near; then I will kill my brother Jacob' " (Genesis 27:41).

Each person is ultimately responsible for his own actions. But home environment often puts an extra burden on kids as they struggle to find their own identity. There is no question that Jacob and Esau would have had an easier time at home if Isaac and Rebekah had presented a united view of parenting. Instead of picking favorites and spoiling one or the other, a system of mutual love and fairness would have been a big help.

In fact, one of the leading obstacles to friendship in marriage is for a Mom and Dad to have different ideas about how to raise the kids.

Marsha and Brian visited with us for over two hours after church one Sunday night. Their marriage was going through intense strain.

"We've been married fifteen years. You would think we wouldn't have such a tough time at it," Marsha sighed.

"I really don't think it's such a big deal," Brian bristled.

They had never been the parents of a junior high girl before. Tina was "almost thirteen" and had recently discovered menstruation, ladies' underwear, and boys (but not necessarily in that order). She now had a boyfriend who enjoyed calling her on the phone almost every night. The phone calls were not very private, not very long, and not very deep . . . but they greatly distressed Marsha.

"Tina doesn't even know how to control her feelings about her horse, let alone some boy." Marsha held back the tears. "We don't even know this guy. I mean, he's on the baseball team, he's in the eighth grade, and he has 'awesome eyes that just make me melt.' Other than that he's a stranger."

But Brian countered, "Hey, Tina's one smart kid. She works hard around the house. She always gets top grades. She's on the student council. We've got to trust her judgment sometimes. Besides she needs to know that we are on her side."

Marsha jumped in, "Restricting her visits with this guy does not mean we are rejecting her."

"Yes, but if we start driving barriers between us now, she won't want to come to us later on when the situation is really critical," Brian reasoned.

Marsha and Brian left us that night feeling distant from one another because their ideas of how to raise Tina remained miles apart.

BIBLICAL BASICS ABOUT KIDS

The problem of how to raise the kids has so decisive an effect on marital harmony that we want to take two chapters to deal with the subject. The place to start is to review the biblical basics about kids.

WHAT ARE KIDS FOR ANYWAY?

"To keep the earth populated with humans."
"To teach their folks patience and long-suffering."
"To provide fun."
"To keep us from being too self-centered."
"To let us experience through them all the things we missed out on as kids."
"To take care of us in our old age."
"To keep us working hard through a lot of otherwise boring years."
"To keep us on our spiritual toes, trusting in the Lord."

What are kids for? How would you answer the question? It probably depends on which day you were asked.

HOW LONG DOES IT TAKE TO RAISE KIDS?

We're not sure. Our oldest is twenty-five . . . and he still needs Mom and Dad at times. Humanettes can be a rather helpless lot. In all the animal kingdom, human babies are the most pitiful. It takes twenty years before most are able to provide for their own food and shelter, and some never learn how to properly dress themselves. Parenting, to some degree, is a lifetime commitment. Remember, it was the Lord who created us this way.

HOW MUCH DOES IT COST TO RAISE KIDS?

You've seen the startling figures that some computer has projected showing the hundreds of thousands of dollars it takes to raise just one child. But those projections do not do justice to the expense. The truth of the matter is that kids will probably cost you all the financial, emotional, physical, social, and spiritual resources you have at your disposal. There will be more than a few days that you feel close to bankruptcy in each of those areas.

The Bible presents an honest view of raising children. There are times of sorrow and disappointment. Eli the prophet, who was little Samuel's teacher, had to face the fact that his own sons were "worthless men; they did not know the Lord" (1 Samuel 2:12). David suffered the extreme grief of losing his son, even though Absalom died trying to kill his father and overthrow his kingdom. "O my son Absalom, my son, my son Absalom! Would I had died instead of you, O Absalom, my son, my son!" (2 Samuel 18:33)

And certainly it was agony at the edge of endurance for Mary to stand by and watch Jesus be crucified (John 19:26). But the Scriptures are also vivid concerning the joys of raising children. Psalm 127:3-5 is a good example:

> Behold, children are a gift of the Lord;
> The fruit of the womb is a reward.
> Like arrows in the hand of a warrior,
> So are the children of one's youth.
> How blessed is the man whose quiver is full of them;
> They shall not be ashamed,
> When they speak with their enemies in the gate.

We Must View Each Child As a Gift from the Lord

Are you gifted parents? Of course you are. When the Lord sent your children to you, He was delivering special gifts to you. They will remain His presents to you all the days of your life.

What are the qualities of a good gift?

SOMETHING YOU DO NOT DESERVE

It was occupation day at the pre-school, and we sat across the courtyard watching the program. Mr. Markus walked up to the front of the assembly wearing the uniform of his occupation as a Los Angeles County fireman. The four-year-olds were in awe. One little boy named Timmy jumped to his feet and pointed enthusiastically. "That's my Dad! That's my Dad! Hi, Dad!"

The same scene has been repeated in each of our lives. What did Mr. Markus have to do to receive such admiration and honor? Nothing. He was Dad. That was enough. Not one of us deserves the honor a little child bestows on Mom and Dad. But then, that's what good gifts are like.

SOMETHING YOU COULD NEVER AFFORD

A good gift is something you would really like to have but could never afford to get for yourself. If only the rich could have children, most of the creative, dynamic people on earth would never have seen the light of day. In a day of planned parenting and genetic engineering, we are in danger of completely forgetting the Lord's control over the size of families. Sometimes He throws a surprise party and gives us a little gift when we least expect it.

A two-child family in modern America is a nice unit. All four of you can fit nicely into even a compact car. A three-bedroom house or apartment is not impossible to find. There is always an equal number of parents and children to attend ballet performances or little league games. Even a small kitchen table has room for four, and a medium-sized tent can hold the whole family on vacation.

For years we operated with this "perfect" sized family unit, believing that we really couldn't afford to have more children. It came as a complete surprise when the Lord informed us when our oldest two were sixteen and thirteen that He had another gift for us.

Aaron has been a delight to us for over nine years, a surprise gift we can't imagine how we ever got along without.

SOMETHING THAT FITS YOU PERSONALLY

What do you do with that shirt or blouse that is such a horrid color? I mean, you want to wear it because it was a gift, but you really can't imagine any place appropriate. A good gift fits you exactly. "It really looks like me, doesn't it?" we gush.

"I don't know where she gets it," Marie's mother shook her head and exclaimed as she staggered down the supermarket aisle.

She had a point. Little Marie's Mom and Dad are both goal-oriented, extremely disciplined business executives. Every decision is calculated, rehearsed, enacted with precision. The late fall of 1983 was to be a time when the company re-tooled two of their biggest factories, and sales were scheduled to be low. So Marie's Mom and Dad decided it would be a good time to have a child and let Mom take a maternity leave. The timing was almost perfect: one week after the Ohio plant shut down, Marie was born.

The day she was brought home from the hospital a carefully prepared daily schedule was posted on the refrigerator, spelling out exactly what should be done, at what time, and by whom. That list remained on the polished almond door for over four months, and never once did anything go according to schedule.

Marie is a free spirit. She seems to operate by inspiration and instinct. Logic appears to have little value to her. Much to her parents' amazement, sitting down and trying to discuss something with her accomplishes nothing at all. At first, it might seem like little Marie does not fit her family at all.

But that's not what her parents say.

"I think she's helped us to loosen up," her dad told us. "We don't worry much about schedules, 'quality time,' and a list of priorities. Marie bounces through life dragging us along and we have found we love the unpredictable adventures."

The Lord knew just the right gift to give. Marie fits in with a splash, thank you.

SOMETHING THAT BRINGS YOU JOY FOR A LONG TIME

Janet has a delightful looking animal that stares down at us from the top of her dresser. His name is Thomas Woof. He was just a silly, spur-of-the-moment present one Valentine's Day. But he can put a smile on our faces every time we see his cross-eyed smile looking down at us. Good gifts keep on bringing joy.

Yesterday we had a Bly doubleheader. We had to attend two baseball games. At 3:15 Aaron's Little League team (the Ameron Mets) faced their dreaded rivals (the Burger Barn Dodgers) in four innings of hard fought ball to determine the sole leader in the National League.

A walked-in run in the bottom of the fourth decided the victory in favor of the Mets. It was a thrilling game.

Then at 6:45 we drove eight miles to watch Russell's softball team play for the league championship. A wild throw from shortstop to home in the bottom of the seventh proved to be the winning run for his team. It was a thrilling game.

Russell is twenty-five . . . Aaron is nine. We've watched Russ play ball for almost twenty years. We figure Aaron will be playing baseball for another thirty. That will mean fifty years of attending ball games and rooting on the kids.

A good gift brings you joy for a long, long time.

WE SHOULD VIEW CHILDREN AS REWARDS

The Psalmist said the "fruit of the womb is a reward." A reward is a gift offered for some special service or extraordinary behavior. Wages are compensation for doing what is expected of you. Rewards, like bonuses, are for that extra service beyond ordinary duty.

The Lord certainly has other ways of rewarding those who for one reason or another are unable to have children. Yet the giving of children is certainly one of His most common ways. Here are some specific ways we are rewarded through our children.

ADDITIONAL PAIRS OF EYES

Children view the world from their own special perspective.

Aaron came into the house and announced, "I don't want to play in my sandbox anymore."

"Why?" we asked. "Because there is a big old worm out there and he keeps sticking out his tongue at me."

We stood staring for a minute; then it hit us . . . a snake! It was a graphic description from the creative eye of a three-year-old.

LIVE-IN REMINDERS OF GENERATIONS TO COME

Children are live-in reminders that we must build a world that will last beyond our generation. We are now busy struggling to help put our second through college. Then in nine more years, Aaron will hit the campus. We want our children trained, educated, prepared to meet the world out there. We've got to vote, be active in civic affairs, get those new schools built. Our grandkids will need good facilities. Kids keep our vision from being single generational.

CLOSE RELATIONSHIPS WITH MULTI-TALENTED INDIVIDUALS

We are rewarded by close relationships with multi-talented individuals who enjoy sharing their talents.

In our den hangs an original oil painting of an amateur rodeo bull-rider trying to make it to the buzzer. Hardly anyone comes over to the house who doesn't get a tour of our original "Russell." No, no, not *Charles* Russell . . . *Russell* Bly. We have four of Russ's paintings and can hardly wait for another.

PEOPLE TO HOLD US ACCOUNTABLE

We are rewarded by having other people live close enough to us to hold us accountable for our actions, words, and ideas.

"Dad, you're always saying the Bible is complete in itself, and there is to be no more revelation, right? Well, this kid at school says his church believes in some book that was found in New York about one hundred and fifty years ago. How can you be so sure that they are wrong?" It took us three hours one night to explain to thirteen-year-old Michael how we knew from Scriptures that the Bible is complete in itself. Of course, we had been dogmatically telling him that for years. He wanted more. He wanted a careful explanation.

OPPORTUNITIES TO ENJOY THE SUCCESSES OF OTHERS

We are rewarded by being able to enjoy fully the success of others in areas where we never succeeded. The whistle blew and the runners sprinted across the park, each hoping to be victorious. The winner among the five- to seven-year-old boys was . . . Aaron Bly. As far as we can tell he was the first Bly boy to win a foot race since 1929. You should have seen the celebration. You would have thought he won the Olympics.

OPPORTUNITIES TO BE HEROES

The two boys sat on our front step.

"Aaron, I saw your Mom and Dad on TV last night."

"Oh, yeah. Well," he paused, "you know, my folks are famous."

"Hey, my dad once caught a foul ball hit by Steve Garvey and they showed the whole thing on the Saturday Game of the Week."

"Really?"

"Yeah."

"Wow, Randy, your Dad is even more famous than mine," Aaron gasped.

"I know," Randy beamed, "I know."

WE SHOULD VIEW CHILDREN AS ARROWS

Psalm 127:4 said, "Like arrows in the hand of a warrior, so are the children of one's youth."

The analogy is a fairly simple one. The scene goes like this. You are an old man. An enemy of yours shows up at the front door and makes threatening remarks. Suddenly your twelve strong, grown sons appear at the door behind you. Now your enemy changes his tune and sheepishly slips out of the yard and down the trail. That scene might be a little hard to apply in your life, but examine all the implications.

ARROWS OF PHYSICAL PROTECTION

Children are "arrows" that can provide physical protection.

Russ and Mike, like their Dad, stand at 6'2" and weigh more than 200 pounds. Steve had to spend the night in the hospital, and as Janet said good night, he sounded worried. "Hey it's dark out there in the parking lot; are you going to be all right?"

"With these two guys with me?" she pointed to Russ and Mike. "I've got more bodyguards than Princess Di."

Children as arrows.

ARROWS OF COMPANIONSHIP

Children are "arrows" that provide companionship. Margerie apologized to our Sunday school class for being late. "My daughter, Patty, stopped by last night and we had a wonderful visit but we stayed up past midnight."

"What did you talk about?" we asked.

"For the first three hours she told me how hard it was for her to be twenty-five and single and out on her own; and for the second three hours I told her how hard it had been for me to be twenty-five and single and out on my own."

Children as arrows.

ARROWS OF SOCIAL ACCEPTANCE

Children are "arrows" that can provide social acceptance.

Folks in the Lakeview district were somewhat suspicious when the Vietnamese family moved into the neighborhood. They were an unknown minority. The language seemed impossible to decipher. The customs were strange. People who had claimed to be quite unprejudiced suddenly had doubts about accepting the likes of the Nguyen family.

But their children settled into school quickly. Chin Thi, the oldest, won the junior high spelling bee in the seventh grade and was elected student body president in the eighth. After Chin Thi came Connie, Cuong, Huy, Kim, Binh, and Elizabeth. All seven have served as student body president of Immanuel Junior High. Mr. and Mrs. Nguyen are respected members of the Lakeview district these days.

Children as arrows.

ARROWS OF SPIRITUAL PROTECTION

Children as "arrows" can provide spiritual protection as well.

The battle around us is definitely a spiritual one. Paul said that "Our struggle is not against flesh and blood, but against the rulers, against the powers, against the world forces of this darkness, against the spiritual forces of wickedness in the heavenly places" (Ephesians 6:12).

As Christian parents we spend so much time trying to teach spiritual truth to our children we sometimes forget that as they trust in Christ they become little warriors in their own right in this great spiritual battle, too.

Eight-year-old Rachael bounded into the house and announced to her parents, "The Lord answered my prayers!"

With condescending smiles they asked, "What prayers, honey?"

"I prayed that Mr. Rodney would not beat up Mrs. Rodney, and he didn't," she beamed.

"What?" they gasped.

"Well, my friend Felicia Rodney said that her Dad always gets drunk and comes home and beats up on her Mom. So I just prayed that he wouldn't do it. The Lord answered my prayers."

"You mean Mr. Rodney didn't come home drunk?"

"Felicia said he got arrested for drunk driving and was put in jail. See, the Lord answered my prayer. Mrs. Rodney didn't get beat up."

A coincidence you say? Only if you can give scriptural evidence that the Lord doesn't listen to the prayers of children.

Children as arrows.

The very first step in building a united view of parenting must be for Mom and Dad to review the joys, delights, and purposes God had in mind when He sent us this crew we call "the kids."

No matter what age your children might be, it's a good idea to sit down and take plenty of time with the following study guide.

"THANK-THE-LORD-FOR-KIDS" SURVEY

1. Child's full name: _____

   Why did we give this child this *particular* full name?

2. The different nicknames we have given this child over the years:

3. The favorite present we received from this child:

   The occasion of the gift:

4. An occasion when one of us said, "That's *my* kid!"

5. The planning we did for this child's birth:

   The surprises this child has brought into our lives:

6. A positive thing this child has added to our lives that we might have missed if he/she had not been a part of our family:

7. The memories brought back when we pour over the family photo album (or cardboard box crammed with pictures) and look at all the pictures we have of this child:

8. The special vocabulary of this child . . . and the words or phrases that will always remind us of this child:

9. The things this child is really good at:

   How many did you teach him? How many seem to be natural talents? How many have no precedent in either parent?

10. A spiritual lesson we have learned from this child, . . . a spiritual truth brought home to us by what this child has said or done:

Do the exercise slowly.

Make sure both parents participate.

Do a complete, individual study for each child.

Finish your time together by reading again Psalm 126:3-5 and have some prayer of thanksgiving for the special people the Lord selected to be your children.

6

Don't Ask Dad . . . Ask Mom!

"What are you doing outside?"

"I'm playing."

"It's too late for you to be out. Tomorrow is a school day."

"Mommy said I could."

"She said you could play outside at 8:00 o'clock at night?"

"Yeah, she said I could play until you came home."

"Well, I'm home. Come in right now."

"I have to pick up my toys first."

"Where's your mother?"

"In the house, I guess."

(Front door slams.)

"Honey, did you tell Junior he could play outside this late?"

"Oh, I suppose."

"Suppose? Now listen, I thought we agreed to give him his bath at 7:00 on school nights."

"Right dear, but since he got his homework all done I told him he could play outside until you got home. You did say you would be home by 7:00."

"Well, I was late, just one of those things. But how can we teach this child any discipline if you won't stick by the rules?"

"What rules are those?"

"Rules for raising kids, that's what."

"I didn't know we had any rules."

"Of course we have rules! Junior has to have his bath at 7:00 P.M. sharp, every night, no matter what."

"No matter whether you keep the rules or not—right, dear?"

"Rules, what rules?"

"Rules for getting home when you promise, so dinner won't get cold."

Now we purposely left off the names of this couple. You can pencil in any ones you want. Maybe it sounds like your brother-in-law, or maybe the folks across the street, or perhaps it sounds like something from your own house.

The truth of the matter is, without a united view of parenting it will be extremely difficult to develop a strong friendship with your mate.

WHY DO YOU AND YOUR SPOUSE DISAGREE ON HOW TO RAISE THE CHILDREN?

YOU GREW UP WITH DIFFERENT ROLE MODELS

The way you were raised sets the stage for how you expect things to operate in your own family. If you liked your parental family situation, you will want to copy it when you have your own family. If, on the other hand, you hated the way you were raised, you will try to structure your family just the opposite. Either way, your background dominates the view you have of how family life should progress. The problem comes when you marry someone who grew up in a family environment completely different from yours. Seldom do "his way" and "her way" agree.

In more than twenty-five years of marriage we have seldom, if ever, argued over the role of the father in raising the children. There's a good reason. Janet grew up in a broken home where there was no father for most of her growing up years. She has no background as to what a dad should be like. Whatever Steve does is acceptable.

Oh my, but we've had some real conflicts over what a mother does. Janet has a laid back, hands off, let-the-kids-learn-responsibility-on-their-own type of attitude. Steve is more the strict disciplinarian. For him there is an exact time and place for everything, and all in the family should follow the rules.

We didn't have to search far for that opening illustration.

Why are we that way? Why is it that after all these years we still have conflicts over the role of a mother? Janet's view reflects her mother's attitude, and Steve's his mother's.

Now it doesn't mean that one role is necessarily right and the other necessarily wrong. It just means that you and your mate will have some disagreements over how to raise the kids, and this is the normal, average, usual, to-be-expected behavior.

YOU ARE OF DIFFERENT PERSONALITY TYPES

Call it personality types, temperaments, behavior patterns, or whatever . . . it's all the same. You and your mate have different innate character qualities. Those differences will affect the way you raise children.

Steve is optimistic. He expected his first attempt to write a book to be published. (It was.) He expected to win $2,000 per week for life at a McDonald's contest. (He didn't.) And he keeps thinking that the Seattle Seahawks are going to win the Super Bowl.

Janet is cautious. (She doesn't like the word *pessimistic*; it's too depressing.) A cloud in the sky means that it's going to rain. Slight air turbulence means an imminent airline crash. If Mrs. Southern doesn't smile it means she is upset with us . . . again.

Translated into child-raising it looks like this:

"Honey, we have to buy Aaron a new white shirt for tomorrow's school program," Janet smiles.

"He doesn't like white shirts," Steve frowns.

"I know, but it says right here in the note from the teacher that all the boys must wear blue jeans and white shirts," Janet insists.

"But it's 8:00 o'clock at night. Where are we going to get a shirt at this hour?" Steve snaps.

"Maybe we can make it to the mall. Aaron forgot to give me the note until just a few minutes ago," Janet affirms.

"Hey, his tan shirt . . . you know, the faded one. He can wear that," Steve triumphs.

"You mean the one we bought him last year that has mustard stains on it?" Janet is definitely gathering steam.

"Yeah, it'll work. Why buy a shirt for one day? Besides I'm too tired to go look for a shirt tonight," Steve pleaded.

"Then you give Aaron a bath, wash his hair, and do the dishes . . . while I run to the mall and find him a shirt. A white shirt means a white shirt," Janet blasts.

"White, light tan, it can't make that much difference," Steve sounds forceful, but desperate.

"I am *not* going to be known as the mother who sent her kid to the program in a stained tan shirt. Now, don't get any shampoo in Aaron's eyes. You know how he screams when that happens," she commands and heads for the front door.

"Wait!" Steve calls in defeat, "What size does he wear? I'll go get the shirt."

YOU HAVE DIFFERENT FAMILY PURPOSES IN MIND

What is the purpose for your family?

"Purpose?" you ask. "We are supposed to have a purpose?"

The truth of the matter is, you have a purpose, whether you have ever talked about it or not.

For instance, Mom could view the purpose of the family as this: to create a healthy environment in which to raise the children and help them develop their God-given gifts and talents to their full potential. Dad's job is therefore seen as a tool to help achieve this important goal.

Dad, on the other hand, could view his job as the central element in the family purpose. Therefore, the wife and kids should be doing all they can to see that Dad does well at work. That means they not only encourage him, but they try to remove any extra elements of stress that might be placed on him at home.

"When are these kids going home? It's almost 7:00," he says.

"Oh, they're not going home until tomorrow morning. Sissy is having a slumber party," she says.

"What? Here?" he says.

"That did seem like a good place for her to have it," she says.

"But . . . but . . . I'm tired. You know how stressed-out I've been at work. Besides, tomorrow is a school day," he says.

"The teachers are having some sort of in-service training. There's no school tomorrow. It's a good chance for Sissy to get to know the neighbor who moved in last week," she says.

"But what about me?" he says.

"Oh, you can meet her too," she says.

"You don't understand; I need a little peace and quiet," he says.

"And you don't understand; there are other people in this family," she says.

Obviously there are two different family purposes in conflict here.

YOU VIEW PARENTING FROM DIFFERENT PERSPECTIVES

You and your spouse view parenting from different perspectives: short-term goals versus long-term goals.

It is a weakness that can strike both husband and wife from time to time. It is a poor response no matter who instigates it. We look for the quickest, easiest solution to the immediate problem, without thinking about the long-term effect of such actions on our kids.

One parent may see the short-sightedness of such action, but the other may not. You've had such an experience.

"I don't want to eat at that #$%*! taco place again," Junior blurts out.

"Don't you ever, *ever*, use that word again!" Dad shouts.

"What word?" Junior quizzes.

"You know what word. If I hear you use that again, I'll stop this car, pull off my belt, and tan your hide. Do you understand?" Dad barks.

"Honey, why don't you tell him why that word makes you so upset?" Mom suggests.

"Because I'm driving through rush hour traffic, that's why," Dad justifies.

Dad felt that a severe threat would keep Junior's speech within bounds. Mom wanted an explanation that would curb Junior's speech in the long run.

We'd like to think that parents are too wise to let this happen. We'd like to say we can compartmentalize our lives and separate our emotions, feelings, and actions. But the truth is, if we're struggling in one relationship it won't be long until we are struggling in all of them. That's why we always complain, "Why does everything go wrong at once!"

Everything goes wrong at once because everything is connected.

Mom has been asking to go to the new department store. She is anticipating a leisurely stroll through brand new merchandise. There are a few things they need to get—a wedding gift for her husband's brother and a light fixture for the dining room. So Dad promises that they will spend Saturday shopping together.

But when the day comes, Hubby's old pickup isn't running so he borrows her car to go fishing with a couple of the fellas from work. "We can go some time next week."

Sometime around two o'clock Junior asks if he and his friends can use Dad's golf clubs out in the backyard. Normally Mom would have said no, but . . . normally, she wouldn't have been so angry at Dad either. "If he doesn't intend to stick around on Saturdays then he will have to face the consequences." She lets Junior use the clubs.

Dad, of course, will be furious. Mom will still be angry. And Junior, well, he will get shot down in the crossfire.

WHAT ARE THE MAJOR SOURCES OF PARENTAL DISUNITY?

Several aspects of child-raising create discord between parents, unless they are discussed beforehand.

DISCIPLINE

Parents sometimes have a problem deciding which punishment fits the crime committed. Justice is finding the right punishment.

If Junior destroys—quite by accident—an iron that Mom snagged up at a garage sale for $2.00 . . . what should be the punishment?

If Junior destroys—quite by accident—a 1942 Lionel Train caboose that Dad snagged at a garage sale for $2 . . . what should be the punishment?

It just might be that Dad thinks the punishment for crime #2 should be considerably greater than for crime #1.

Parental discipline is an assumed truth of Scripture.

"It is for discipline that you endure; God deals with you as with sons; for what son is there whom his father does not discipline?" (Hebrews 12:7)

"Furthermore, we had earthly fathers to discipline us, and we respected them; shall we not much rather be subject to the Father of spirits, and live?" (Hebrews 12:9)

You and your mate should sit down and discuss discipline once more. The following might be a format to follow:

PUNISHMENT

Level 1:   The least serious infractions of family rules. Acceptable punishment at this level includes:
    a.
    b.
    c.

Level 2:   Moderate infractions. Minor things repeated without correction, more deliberate actions involving others and having more lasting consequences. Punishment at this level includes:
    a.
    b.
    c.

Level 3:   Serious infractions. Open, willful disobedience against known family rules. Actions that threaten peace and unity. Punishment here includes:
    a.
    b.
    c.

"The Biggie":   The ultimate act of willful rebellion against parents
                 and against God. There will be no greater punish-
                 ment inflicted.
                 a.
                 b.
                 c.

Fill in appropriate types of punishment at each level. For instance,
where does sending the child to his room fit in? How about the horrible punishment of turning off the TV for a whole day? And what
about spanking? Should it be used? When? Once you have these
filled in, decide who is responsible for carrying out the punishment at
each level. Mom? Dad? Both?

After reaching some agreement on these things, list the types of
crimes that fit each of the categories.

Level 1 crimes include such things as:

Level 2 crimes include such things as:

Level 3 crimes include such things as:

The Biggie includes such things as:

Where does punching little sister fit in? Where does kicking big
brother? What about cussing out the neighbor kid? Cussing out
Mom? Give plenty of examples so that you will have a good idea
about united discipline.

A mom and dad who have worked through these discussions are
well on their way to becoming best friends.

MONEY

How much money should Junior have? How much should he be
allowed to spend without Mom and Dad's prior approval?

We should pay attention to the warning of Scripture: "But those
who want to get rich fall into temptation and a snare and many foolish and harmful desires which plunge men into ruin and destruction.

For the love of money is a root of all sorts of evil"
(1 Timothy 6:9-10a).

We do our children a great favor when we guide them in the use of money.

Here's one plan that might work for you.

1. Decide on an appropriate allowance for each age group. The correct amount will depend upon your personal budget and a child's maturity in handling money.

Age	Dollar Amount
0-2	
3-4	
5-6	
7-8	
9-10	
11-12	
13-14	
15-16	
17-18	

Fill out the whole chart, even if your children are quite young. It will give you a good perspective. Of course, you might have to change it as times and economic conditions alter.

2. List some appropriate family responsibilities that go along with this allowance. Again, take each age level and jot down the type of household jobs that would be reasonable to expect at that age—everything from picking up the clothes in their rooms to mowing the lawn and babysitting the younger children.

3. Go back through the age breakdown one more time and write down how much money the child is allowed to spend per week without your supervision. Little eight-year-old Junior may have a $400 savings account, but you may decide to tell him he can only spend fifty cents a week without consulting you first.

Now you've got a united view of handling money with your kids.

BEDTIME

When should each child go to bed? Sounds simple. Why do so many moms and dads still argue over it? It shouldn't be merely what is most convenient—or easiest.

Here are some steps parents can use to establish some general rules for each child.

1. Write down the normal time Junior needs to leave the house in the morning: say, 7:40 A.M. on school days.

2. Subtract the normal time it takes Junior to get up, get dressed, and eat a well-balanced breakfast: say, 1 hour . . . so Junior should get up at 6:40.

3. Subtract the amount of time Junior needs to sleep in order to feel his best the next day: say, 10 hours . . . which means Junior must be asleep by 8:40 P.M.

4. Subtract how long it takes Junior to get to sleep after you tuck him in and pray with him: say, 20 minutes . . . which means Junior's bedtime is 8:20 P.M.

5. Then subtract the amount of time it takes Junior to take his bath, brush his teeth, and get ready for bed: you will have arrived at Junior's bath time. For example, if he likes to play in the tub, and it takes a total of 40 minutes, bath time is 7:30 P.M.

Now you and your spouse agree on Junior's bedtime, and Junior knows there is no use appealing to the other parent, because both of you are in it together.

Of course, Sissy's age and needs might be different, so her bedtime would be different.

FREEDOM

From time to time, there will be differences of opinion between Mom and Dad over how much freedom each child should have.

When is Junior old enough to go over and play in the neighbor's back yard alone? When can Sissy go to a slumber party? When can Junior go hiking in the woods with just the other fellas? And the *ultimate* . . . when will we allow Sissy to go out on a date?

We keep thinking we will have those problems solved by the time the kids reach that age . . . we seldom do.

You can mutually agree upon some general guidelines, realizing that each child must be treated somewhat differently. Perhaps it's best to start at the far end and work backwards. At what age will you consider your child to be on his own and responsible enough to make decisions and decide how to use his time? Twenty-one? Nineteen? Seventeen? You will need to decide.

Then push back through the years, listing the types of things your child will have the freedom to decide at each age: Nineteen? Seventeen? Fifteen? Thirteen? Eleven? Nine? Seven? Five? Three?

At what age does your child decide, on his own, where he wants to go on Friday night? When does he decide, on his own, whether he wants to keep taking piano lessons? When does he decide, on his own, what kind of music to listen to? When does he decide, on his own, what to order at the restaurant? When does he decide, on his own, what color to paint his room?

Dialogue will help clarify the wheres and whys of your points of contention. And any time you must turn down a child's request, you can present a united view of when he will achieve the freedom he requests.

FRIENDS

From time to time, Mom and Dad may have disagreements over who will be good friends for their children.

There's no way to avoid the scriptural mandate, "Do not be deceived: 'Bad company corrupts good morals' " (1 Corinthians 15:33).

Mom and Dad may want to adopt some guidelines. These are a few you might include.

- Friends should not be a detriment to our child's spiritual life.
- Friends should not be a detriment to our child's moral life.

• Friends should not be selected merely to be a convenience to the parents.
• Friends should never be selected in a way that teaches racial, economic, or social prejudice to our children.

You can add other, more personal guidelines to the list.

GRANDPARENTS

You can't deny it. Sometimes the way your in-laws (or your own parents) treat the kids is downright destructive to family unity.

But the inter-generational bond can be a beautiful thing.

"Grandchildren are the crown of old men," Proverbs 17:6 teaches. "A good man leaves an inheritance to his children's children," Proverbs 13:22 observes.

As Mom or Dad and also daughter or son, you have to balance the dual interaction with both generations. Like most other points of conflict in parenting, much can be solved by sitting down and calmly talking it out. Use the guidelines below as a checklist.

Give each of the grandparents equal honor. Make sure all grandparents are given equal honor in the sight of the children, so that you can obey the commandment, "Honor your father and your mother" (Exodus 20:12).

Don't try to give each grandparent equal time. Grandparents need not be given exactly equal time. The set that lives across town is going to see the kids lots more than the set that lives across the country. There should be no guilt in that.

Sometimes certain environments are better for the growth and maturity of children, even if all grandparents live close by. Husband and wife together must decide just how much time, for instance, the children should spend with an alcoholic grandfather. Always equal honor, not always equal time.

Help your children get to know their grandparents. Work at helping the kids really get to know their grandparents. Spend time looking at family photos and talking about "olden days" with them before they go to visit grandma and grandpa. When the whole family is together, strike up conversations about days past. Don't let the kids miss out on the treasures another generation has to offer.

Agree ahead of time about how much spoiling you are going to allow. You and your spouse should agree ahead of time as to the amount of spoiling you are going to allow the grandparents to do. Kids need to be spoiled a little and grandparents seem to be naturals at it. But don't lose control of parenting. It's still your responsibility.

FUTURE GOALS AND CAREERS

"Mom thinks I should study art, but Dad wants me to teach math . . . just like he does." Of course, the younger your children are, the easier it is. Yet it's tough trying to figure out their careers. You want them to have jobs that are financially stable, to be prominent in the fields they have elected, to be content—but still to know what it's like to put in a hard day's work. So you make some plans for them, you follow some dreams, you sacrifice funds and time, and . . . they end up doing whatever they want anyway.

Well, that's the way it sometimes seems. But it's not entirely true. Parents who are united in their encouragement of the child often find themselves being of great influence in their child's career. The secret is to help him find how God is leading him, and then to provide opportunities for him to grow in that direction.

Proverbs 22:6 says, "Train up a child in the way he should go, even when he is old he will not depart from it." Train up a child to use his God-given gifts, talents, and ministries . . . and he will find true satisfaction in that service and continue in that direction all of his life.

Sit down as husband and wife and discuss the following:

1. At the end of our lives here on earth, in those last few days as we look at our children, what factors will indicate to us that we have been successful in child-raising? How rich they are? How famous they are? How powerful they are? Or how much they love their family? How much they love and worship the Lord? What they have

achieved in life that has lasting spiritual value? How much biblical wisdom they have on their own?

2. Now, as you have sorted out priorities for your children together, pledge yourselves to encourage them to develop those gifts, talents, and ministries that have the best chance of developing the very factors that you have decided are of utmost importance in the long run.

SPIRITUAL INSTRUCTION

Often in a marriage there is conflict over just how much spiritual instruction is needed and who should be in charge of seeing that it takes place.

The scriptural text is fairly straightforward: "And fathers, do not provoke your children to anger; but bring them up in the discipline and instruction of the Lord" (Ephesians 6:4).

Again, Mom and Dad must sit down and agree on some guidelines ahead of time. Here are some things to discuss.

- Is the church supposed to be the primary source of our children's spiritual instruction? What does the Bible say about the parent's role?

   Proverbs 6:20 says, "My son, observe the commandment of your father, and do not forsake the teaching of your mother."
- Who should take the primary role of spiritual leadership with the children?
- What is the minimum amount of spiritual knowledge we would like our children to have at age five? Ten? Fifteen? Twenty? How can we insure that they gain this knowledge?
- When should the kids attend the morning worship service? The evening worship service? Be allowed to go forward on their own at an altar call? Be baptized? Receive communion? Go on a missions trip? Teach or help in vacation Bible school?

SEEING EYE TO EYE

"We just don't see eye to eye on raising the kids!"

It's a common lament. It's difficult, if not impossible to go to bed as the best of friends if you have just spent the past four hours pointing out why he is a lousy father or why she is just not cutting it as a mother. There has to be a united view of parenting. Here are three prerequisites you cannot ignore.

Pray for your children every day, together. No shortcuts here. Each child deserves to be mentioned in prayer by Mom and Dad every day. To do less is to grossly underestimate the difficulty kids face in learning to be godly in an ungodly world.

Agree that the Bible will be your ultimate guide for parenting. Get all the help you can from the books and speakers of the day. Bring to your parenting struggles all the wisdom you have discovered as you yourself grew up. *But . . .* hold onto only those things that are compatible with the teaching of Scripture. Agree that you will never claim to be doing things "Dad's way" or "Mom's way"—rather, the Lord's way.

Pledge yourselves to treat each child as an individual. Kids don't come in sets—not even twins or triplets do. Each one is a special, God-designed person. Each one is a complex, mysterious, untapped reservoir of tremendous potential. Help them to appreciate their family similarities, and their many differences.

"Dad, I've just got to stay up later tonight," Aaron squealed.

"What's the problem, you behind on your homework?" Steve questioned.

"Oh no," eight-year-old Aaron's voice was anxious and high-pitched. "It's half time and the Lakers are only ahead by four lousy points. If Magic doesn't start hitting from the outside, and if Worthy can't drive in to the basket any better than in the first half, they might lose the game."

"Did Mom say you could stay up?"

"No, she said it was my bedtime, but she doesn't understand basketball," he complained.

"Well," Steve added with finality, "I agree completely with your Mother. You'll just have to read about the results in the sports page tomorrow."

"That's not fair," Aaron wailed. "You two are always on the same side!"

Smart kid.

Smart folks.

They are the best of friends.

7

My Mate Is Not Very Spiritual

What in the world did she ever see in the guy in the first place? Of course, they lived in a different era and culture. We can only suppose that it was an arranged marriage. It seems unlikely that she would have volunteered to marry such a man.

We've been told that she was "intelligent and beautiful in appearance." The king called her "blessed and discerning." We know her to be decisive and quick to follow the Lord's leading.

But him? A classic jerk. History records him as "harsh and evil in his dealings." His employees said of him that he was "such a worthless man that no one can speak to him." And his wife had to admit that "folly is with him."

In fact, his name, Nabal, means fool. His wife was Abigail. The story unfolds in 1 Samuel 25.

David and his men had been chased out of Israel by King Saul and were spending their time in the hills beyond Saul's influence. In those same mountains resided the sheep owner, Nabal. He was extremely wealthy and influential. Yet surrounded as he was by the Philistines and Amalekites, it was extremely difficult for him to keep his large flocks safe. But Nabal had good fortune. David and his men were camping nearby, and as a consequence no one dared attack Nabal. It was like having a personal army to keep him safe. And David never demanded anything in return from Nabal.

At shearing season Nabal began to reap huge profits from the sheep. David thought it only right to send some of his men to ask Nabal for supplies. After all, it was difficult feeding so many hungry men.

But Nabal's greedy eye was focused on the bumper crop he had harvested, and he pretended not to know anything about David. He sent David's men away empty-handed and insulted. A horrible miscalculation. David had no intention of seeing his men starve while Nabal grew rich. So David set off to relieve Nabal of everything . . . sheep, belongings, family, hired help, and life.

It was only the quick reaction of Abigail that appeased David. Astute and alert, she not only provided for the needs of David and his men but reasoned with him concerning his plan to put Nabal to death. She made the point with David that the vengeance he had planned would not be in his best interest.

So how *did* Abigail get married to such an insensitive man? Probably through no fault of her own. Nabal, being rich and powerful, would have had his pick of lovely young ladies. Almost any parent would have been eager to tap into his wealth.

We can assume with confidence that Abigail had such an excuse. Most modern couples don't.

Sherry met Tom when they both worked in the Peace Corps. Each was excited to find someone else who had a driving desire to help people in other lands. Sherry saw her work as a direct response to the love she felt for Christ. Tom viewed his efforts as meeting the pressing needs of a crowded, hungry world. The couple married in Ethiopia, and they served six years in Africa. Every day they maintained a tight balance between success and failure, with very little personal time. They returned home fulfilled but exhausted.

Back in the States, they began to develop a less hectic routine. Sherry thought that for sure Tom would now begin to seek spiritual truth. He had always said he wanted to understand her faith better, if he ever had the time.

But that was long ago in the African wilderness. Now he wanted nothing to do with talk about God, acted insulted if she wanted to go to any church functions, and actually ridiculed her faith in front of the children. Tension pushed them both to the exploding point several times.

The Bible calls it "unequally yoked" in the King James Version. The NASB* says, "Do not be bound together with unbelievers; for what partnership have righteousness and lawlessness, or what fellowship has light with darkness?" (2 Corinthians 6:14) The injunction cautions believers: do not marry unbelievers. Some apply this principle to business, ecclesiastical, and other intimate personal relationships. To remain strong in their faith, devotion, and service, Christians must refrain from complex entanglements with people of "the world."

Well, how does all this affect friendship with your mate? It strikes at the deepest possible point in a relationship. Battle over the importance of the Lord in your life is the most devastating factor in destroying a friendship. It is so serious that we are not given any options. Christians should never marry non-Christians. Children should be taught this wisdom from a very early age. There are enough struggles, trials, and sorrows to overcome in order to make a marriage work in our current society. We must spare our children the automatic heartbreaks of an unequally yoked union.

But don't think that because your mate has made some kind of commitment to Christ the problem of being "unequally yoked" no longer applies to you. Although it is true that the basic difference —one spouse being a believer and the other being an unbeliever—is the only one which must be avoided altogether, there are other differences as well that put special strains on a marriage relationship. It is crucial for a couple to admit that difficulties exist before they come to an impasse in their relationship.

Angela was Hispanic. She was also a beautiful Christian young lady who was thoroughly in love. But when Angela's mother and father got together with Bruce's Caucasian parents to plan the wedding, tension mounted. Bruce's parents wanted the wedding in the evening; Angela's insisted it be at twelve noon. His parents wanted a small reception at a local restaurant; hers demanded an eight-hour affair at the Memorial Building. His parents thought three or four attendants would suffice; her parents felt there should be at least eight. Bruce agreed with his parents. Angela sided with hers.

* New American Standard Bible.

The wedding took place, a conglomeration that didn't satisfy either side. That was certainly not their last point of conflict. Bruce and Angela are now wise enough to know that an interracial marriage has certain built-in conflicts. They know a wonderful freedom and equality in their commitment to Jesus Christ, but they continue to face irritations and misunderstandings in their friendship with each other.

Cynthia grew up in East Cleveland. For eighteen years her life was shaped by being a pastor's kid in a large urban area. Then she flew off to school in Tulsa, Oklahoma.

Wayne grew up in Marshall, Oklahoma (population 372). During his first eighteen years, his experiences centered around going to rodeos on Saturdays and listening to his father preach on Sundays. Then he rode off to college in Tulsa.

Wayne and Cynthia met in a botany class their freshman year, fell in love during their second year of French, and got married right after their junior year. Everything breezed along until graduation—then fireworks. Cynthia longed for the city. Wayne could hardly wait to get back to the country. He wanted a cabin overlooking a ranch; she wanted a condo overlooking Lake Erie. He liked breakfast early; she preferred a late brunch. He wanted a new pickup; she shopped for a Mercedes. He wanted children right away; she planned a career. Neither one was completely right. Neither one was completely wrong. But neither one wanted to give in. Yet both were Christians, and both had the same racial heritage.

So why did Cynthia fly back to East Cleveland alone? And why did Wayne show up in Marshall without his bride? What happened? Two heartbroken families are wondering.

Lori's conversion was dramatic. While stoned on drugs she fought a guy who came at her with a knife down a dark alley. She tore loose and escaped through a side door where she found herself in the midst of the evening service of Hillside Rescue Mission. Her life was never the same.

Within months she trusted her wasted life to the mercy of Jesus, found help in overcoming her drug dependency, and was trained in computers for an office job. Until she crashed through that door, no one had ever told her plainly about God's love. She had no background in Sunday school, church, the Bible, youth group meetings, or summer camps.

Alan accepted Christ as his Savior in his first grade Sunday school class. He can't remember a year passing without children's church, vacation Bible school, summer camp at Mountain Meadows, and Wednesday youth group Bible studies. After college he got a management job in a growing company. His job was to supervise all the word processing operations in the marketing department.

That's where Alan and Lori met. Six months later they were happily married. Five years later they were still married, but not so happily.

"Alan just assumes I have all the spiritual background and knowledge that he does. He's always volunteering me for situations I can't handle yet," Lori moans.

"She is always dragging her feet about Christian service," Alan counters. "Sometimes I wonder just what kind of commitment she has."

There is only one "unequally yoked" relationship that we are prohibited from entering. But there are many types of unequal yoking that cause an extra burden on marital friendships. Each type can be overcome, but in no case will it be easy.

What about the clash of two who come from entirely different home environments? A wife from a peaceful, traditional family home, and a husband from a violent or a single parent home? How about a wife from an Arminian, Pentecostal background marrying a man from a Baptist, Calvinistic background? Or a thirty-year-old man who has been married once marrying a twenty-year-old girl who has never dated anyone else?

Apart from our mutual commitment to Christ, there is a sense in which none of us is "equally yoked." We're drawn to mates who provide a change of outlook or opportunity, a diversity. But it would surely help if somebody warned us about the common struggles ahead, so we wouldn't take them all so personally. He doesn't always hate you. She isn't really out to put you in your place. It just takes time for two diverse people to get all the gears of marriage into their proper grooves. As soon as you solve one area of conflict, another one appears.

But no matter what kind of situation you describe for yourself and your mate, the spiritual differences will always cause the most serious division.

MY MATE ISN'T GROWING SPIRITUALLY

CHECK TO SEE THAT YOUR UNDERSTANDING OF THE SITUATION IS ACCURATE

Your first job is to find out if it is really true that your mate isn't growing spiritually. Ask your mate what he thinks about his spiritual progress. It just might be he thinks everything's going along just fine. He may not feel any need to change. And you must consider the possibility that he might be right. It is possible for us to expect too much from others, or to fail to see the whole picture. At times we can be more demanding of our spouses than the Lord.

If your mate feels quite content with his spiritual life, it is important for you to consider the possibility that you are making unreasonable demands. Sometimes frustration over our own spiritual progress makes us lash out at others. In those cases, what we are probably saying is, "If my mate were spiritually stronger, he could make up for my own deficiencies and weaknesses."

However, your mate might very well know that he isn't growing spiritually. He might be just as frustrated as you are.

FIND OUT WHAT YOUR SPOUSE'S MODEL OF SPIRITUALITY IS

Ask your mate to describe his (or her) ideal spiritual example. One source of conflict between mates over spirituality is that each brings to the marriage different ideas of what the ideal Christian husband or wife looks like. It will help your marriage immensely if you and your spouse are united on spiritual goals.

Spend time talking about the Bible character you most admire. Discuss his or her positive qualities. Share why that character is, and is not, like you.

Then exchange ideas regarding the biblical character you would like your mate to be like. "I'd like you to be more like David. Or Samuel. Or Joshua. Or Daniel. Or Sarah. Or Martha. Or Lydia."

Also, share your ideas regarding contemporary role models. What person among your Christian acquaintances would you most like to emulate? What person would you like your spouse to be like? Ask your mate if he thinks your examples are reasonable. Begin to realize that there are diverse biblical examples of spiritually mature believers.

DISCUSS THE OBSTACLES TO SPIRITUALITY YOUR SPOUSE FACES

You and your mate need to discuss the three biggest obstacles that keep him (or her) from times of personal Bible study, prayer, and regular worship attendance.

No one can maintain any level of spiritual growth and maturity without those disciplines. But remember: nagging seldom motivates any mate to spiritual maturity. So find out what things are preventing your mate from building good habits of spiritual discipline. Some things to look for include the following:

- an overload of responsibilities at work
- a lack of any background in building habits that lead to spiritual growth
- an addiction to television, sports, or a hobby
- an inability to relate to the current preacher at your church
- an inability to understand a particular version of the Bible
- an inability to read well
- a fear of public scrutiny
- a sense of being physically worn out
- a sense of being trapped by housework and child-raising

The list goes on and on. Some obstacles we create for ourselves, and some are thrust upon us by others. Either way, they stand as barriers to spiritual growth.

SHARE THE OBSTACLES TO SPIRITUAL GROWTH YOU FACE

Talk with your mate about the obstacles you have in your own life that prevent your spiritual growth. In looking for problems in your mate's spiritual life, you may have discovered some weaknesses in your own. "How can I complain about his irregular Bible study when mine is so haphazard?" you say.

You're right. You can't. Go to your mate and share your own struggles.

ASK YOUR MATE TO HELP YOU OVERCOME THOSE OBSTACLES

Be open and honest. You do not have all the answers to the problems inherent in spiritual growth and discipleship. You both are struggling pilgrims like the rest of us. You both have some strengths and many weaknesses. But you have a desire to be different. With God's grace and your mate's help, you can grow to be more like the Christ you try to follow.

Ask your mate to be just as critical with you as you would like to be with him. Here's how this can work.

Suppose you feel your wife is spending too much time reading romance novels and not enough time in personal Bible study. You could just demand that she stop reading the romances. But that may not be too effective, let alone harmonious or spiritual.

Or you could calmly sit down and talk with her about her "problem." However, she might bring up the fact that you sit around watching westerns on the VCR almost every night. Now you are deadlocked.

The solution is to deal with your own problem first. Ask her to remind you about Bible study. Ask her to help you limit your time in front of the television. Ask her to quiz you on what you have been reading.

When you have been honest and brave enough to do this, you are ready for the next step.

OFFER TO HELP YOUR MATE OVERCOME THE OBSTACLES
TO SPIRITUAL GROWTH HE FACES

"Man, I so appreciate your helping me get back into Bible study. Is there anything I can do to help you?" Now you are on her side. You haven't attacked her from across the battlefield, but instead you are standing alongside her in the trenches, ready to assist where needed.

PRESENT REALISTIC MINISTRY OPPORTUNITIES
THAT WILL CAUSE BOTH OF YOU TO GROW SPIRITUALLY

If your mate's spiritual life is lagging behind, chances are he—or she—won't even recognize spiritual opportunities for service. You can be the eyes for both of you.

One problem to watch out for is the tendency to select ministry opportunities that are geared for your mate's spiritual growth only. For instance, you might sign the two of you up to teach the fourth grade Sunday school class for the summer.

"It will keep him studying," you reason.

But what if you've taught fourth graders off and on for ten or twenty years? For you, it's a piece of cake. For him, it's a nightmare of un-ending pressure. Perhaps teaching the fourth grade class is not an especially good choice. Look for something that will cause both of you to grow.

PRAY CONSISTENTLY FOR YOUR MATE

Pray when your mate isn't growing. Pray when your mate is grow-ing. Notice how Paul prays for his friends in Ephesians 1:17-19: "[I pray] that the God of our Lord Jesus Christ, the Father of glory, may give to you a spirit of wisdom and of revelation in the knowledge of Him. I pray that the eyes of your heart may be enlightened, so that you may know what is the hope of His calling, what are the riches of the glory of His inheritance in the saints, and what is the surpassing greatness of His power toward us who believe."

Paul's friends in Ephesus needed him to be in prayer about those things. Your best friend needs your prayers as well. If you don't pray for your mate's spiritual growth, who will?

But what about those who find themselves married to a truly non-spiritual person? What if there is no spiritual commitment at all?

GUIDELINES FOR THOSE MARRIED TO A NON-CHRISTIAN

One thing you cannot do.

You can't dump them.

Paul makes that clear in 1 Corinthians 7:10-11: "But to the mar-ried I give instructions, not I, but the Lord, that the wife should not leave her husband, . . . and . . . the husband should not send his wife away. "

Finding yourself married to a non-spiritual mate is not justification for divorce.

So, what can you do?

DETERMINE TO MAKE THE BEST OF YOUR PRESENT SITUATION

Forget about the self-pity. Of course you should have been more discerning. Yes, others probably have an easier road than you. You may regret some decisions of the past. But commit all those conditions to the Lord God. He still has a future in mind for you.

Take stock of what you do have. You still have a mate. You have a powerful, loving, forgiving Lord. You have your own commitment. That's good working material for the potential of exciting surprises yet to come.

At this point you are responsible only for working with what you have. Allow the Lord to use your situation as a showcase for His glory, honor, and power.

ALWAYS KEEP YOUR MATE'S CONVERSION AS YOUR ULTIMATE GOAL

Don't kid yourself. We hear folks say, "My husband isn't very . . . er, religious. But he's a good man!" We rejoice with you in his goodness. But he's either saved or he's unsaved. A person is either born, or he is not born . . . no one is in between. So it is with the kingdom of God. Be honest. Admit, at least to yourself, that your mate is unsaved.

If this is your situation, not a day should go by without your consciously thinking of your mate's need for salvation. Don't be satisfied with a peaceful family, an affluent life-style, or a lasting marriage. Keep your focus on your mate's conversion. Otherwise, you withhold from him your ultimate proof of love. That's something a best friend would never do.

DO EVERYTHING IN YOUR POWER TO PRESERVE FAMILY UNITY

Don't allow religious activity to place a barrier between you and your mate. Yes, you must live in obedience to the Scriptures. Yes, you must continue in your study, prayer, and worship. Yes, you will need some time to use your spiritual gifts. But you do not have to do everything. If your mate is unconverted, the Lord has given you a huge spiritual ministry right there at home. Don't neglect it. It may be something you alone can accomplish.

SEEK CREATIVE ALTERNATIVES TO TIME CONFLICTS

At times, your church meeting will be scheduled for the same evening your mate wants to go to the ball game. Try to resolve schedule conflicts in such a way that everyone wins. Spend extra time with your mate on the days your ministry calls you away from home. Be quick to support your mate's activities on days when there is no conflict.

WORK HARD TO FULFILL YOUR BIBLICAL ROLE

When you are without spiritual help from your mate, you are in a tough situation. Yet you can't back away from the Bible's commands for husbands and wives. Work hard to fulfill your biblical role. If you have children, your shining example is more crucial than ever.

NEVER COMPROMISE CLEAR BIBLICAL TRUTH

Preserving family peace is not the highest goal above all goals. If your spouse makes demands that would force you to disobey the Bible's teachings, you must refuse. But you can refuse with love and a quiet, reasonable explanation.

MAINTAIN A CONCENTRATED PRAYER LIFE FOR YOUR MATE

Everyone should pray for his (or her) mate. It's what best friends do. But if you have an unsaved mate, he (or she) needs your prayers more than ever. Pray daily for your mate's safety. Pray that your mate will have the strength to overcome temptation. Pray that your mate might, on this very day, be open to receiving spiritual truth.

TRUST GOD'S TIMING

Of course, you want your mate to be saved instantly. So does the Lord—but at times He waits to bring that about. There may be a reason beyond your own needs, even beyond the needs of your family, that calls for you to endure a season of waiting.

The prodigal son in Luke 15 didn't repent and head home until he discovered the vanity of a life spent pursuing pleasure.

Paul didn't believe in Christ in Acts 7, even though he had witnessed the powerful preaching of Stephen. Remembering his mindless persecution of the church in those early days kept him humble the rest of his life.

Jacob grew up in the shadow of the faithfulness of Isaac, yet it wasn't until he fled for his life that he came to acknowledge the Lord God.

Trust that God will save your mate at the very earliest possible moment compatible with his spiritual good.

Chances are you and your mate could spend the whole evening just talking about your spiritual differences. It wouldn't be a bad way to spend your time. Don't hide the topic just because you think the two of you won't agree.

Until you get down to the hard rock honesty of your spiritual lives, you really haven't become your mate's very best friend.

8

Complementary Spiritual Growth

She expected her husband to provide for her in the manner to which she was accustomed. After all, she grew up as the daughter of a king. Now, it wasn't that hubby was stingy with the bucks. It was just, well, at times he didn't act very—how shall we put it—royal. He just flat out humiliated her to death with his actions. Take his worship, for instance.

Now it's not that she was against religion. She just thought he should be much more discreet and tasteful in his expressions of worship. Certainly bringing the Ark of God into the new capital city was important, was even an occasion for a national holiday. And to be sure, her husband, as ruler, should have been a part of the procession. But a true king was carried by his servants on a throne when he traveled with crowds of commoners. And he wore his regal robes and armor.

But what did this king do? She could hardly believe it.

"David went and brought up the ark of God from the house of Obed-edom into the city of David with gladness."

"And David was dancing before the Lord with all his might, and David was wearing a linen ephod. So David and all the house of Israel were bringing up the ark of the Lord with shouting and the sound of the trumpet. Then it happened as the ark of the Lord came into the city of David that Michal the daughter of Saul looked out of the window and saw King David leaping and dancing before the Lord; and she despised him in her heart."

"But when David returned to bless his household, Michal the daughter of Saul came out to meet David and said, 'How the king of Israel distinguished himself today! He uncovered himself today in the eyes of his servants' maids as one of the foolish ones shamelessly uncovers himself!' " (2 Samuel 6:12b; 14-16; 20)

David did not worry about his attire. He was quite willing to be counted among the lowly and humble. He celebrated "before the Lord" (v. 21), so he thought only of Him.

David's and Michal's spiritual commitments were not at the same level. Unattended, the conflict brought alienation. The same type of thing happens still.

Marshall is a demonstrative guy. He yells the loudest at ball games, cries the loudest at funerals, and complains the loudest at church board meetings. He is the one guy you know is listening to the morning sermon, because he punctuates the message with a loud "Amen!" or "Hallelujah!" or "Preach on, brother!" Most of us have gotten used to Marshall's comments. All except Cecelia. She is Marshall's wife.

Cecelia spent the first five years of marriage trying to refine Marshall's style of worship. She had to give up in despair. He didn't give her any choice. Now Cecelia sits in the back row of the balcony every Sunday, while Marshall sits up in the second row, right in front of the pulpit. Even now, she winces when his "Praise the Lord!" breaks the otherwise silent response of the congregation.

Both Cecelia and Marshall want their spiritual lives to grow. It's just that they seem to be growing in opposite directions.

In the last chapter we dealt with situations in which only one person in the marriage was concerned about growing spiritually. What about when both members desire spiritual growth? What can they do to see that such growth strengthens, rather than fractures, a friendship in marriage?

TEN PROJECTS THAT WILL KEEP YOU BOTH GROWING SPIRITUALLY

Sometimes we don't know how to ensure simultaneous spiritual growth with our mate. Below are some ideas.

SPEND AN EVENING DISCUSSING YOUR
SPIRITUAL SIMILARITIES AND DIFFERENCES

Let your mate know clearly that you do not expect his spiritual life to be identical to yours. Show your acceptance of his diversity. The following ideas might be a starting point for your discussion.

• Study Romans 12:3-8 together. Notice what it says about diversity.

> For through the grace given to me I say to every man among you not to think more highly of himself than he ought to think; but to think so as to have sound judgment, as God has allotted to each a measure of faith. For just as we have many members in one body and all the members do not have the same function, so we, who are many, are one body in Christ, and individually members one of another. And since we have gifts that differ according to the grace given to us, let each exercise them accordingly: if prophecy, according to the proportion of his faith; if service, in his serving; or he who teaches, in his teaching; or he who exhorts, in his exhortation; he who gives, with liberality; he who leads, with diligence; he who shows mercy, with cheerfulness.

• Without consulting each other, list five of your own spiritual strengths and five of your spiritual weaknesses. Then repeat the process, listing your mate's spiritual strengths and weaknesses. Now exchange lists and openly discuss each other's surveys. The goal is to be obedient to Romans 12:3 and to develop an honest view of yourself.
• Jot down three ways your spiritual lives are similar, then jot down three ways your spiritual lives are different. Discuss.
• No matter how often you have talked about it, spend time discussing your spiritual development, or lack of it, as a child. Share when you first learned about God, the church, the Bible, Jesus. Make special notes of the differences in your backgrounds.
• Once again, discuss your individual conversion experiences. How did you come to trust in Jesus Christ as Lord and Savior?

Do you think your different conversion experiences have in any way affected your present spiritual differences? How?

• Spend some good time in prayer together, thanking God for the spiritual life and gifts of your mate. Pledge yourselves before God to assist each other to discover the Lord's best for your lives.

ATTEND A WEEKLY DISCUSSION-ORIENTED BIBLE STUDY TOGETHER

Once a month just won't do. You both need the discipline of regular study. If you attend a study once a month and happen to miss a session, two months will have passed before you return. You can't survive on that kind of spiritual diet.

Make sure it is the kind of study in which you have many opportunities to discuss the spiritual truth you are learning. There is great value in attending classes that are straight teaching from a spiritually knowledgeable source, but we all need as well a regular study where we are free to ask any questions we might have.

Such a study might be held in a home situation on a week night evening. Or it might be held during the Sunday school hour at church. A Bible study group is such a high priority for your spiritual growth—and thus for your friendship in marriage—that you should spend the money and hire a good babysitter for the kids. Scratch off that weeknight for the whole year, and refuse to ever schedule anything that conflicts with the study.

Look for a group that is small enough to get to know and care for each member of the study. Twelve people is the absolute maximum number for such a study, and eight is closer to the ideal. Try to find a group in which each member is open to accepting the other members exactly where they are. Search for a discussion leader who allows each of you to probe, question, doubt, search, and discover.

It might be that you need to start a new study like this in your home. If so, go to your pastor and volunteer to help get such a study going. Work under his guidance and supervision.

We have enjoyed the fact that the Lord has allowed our spiritual lives to grow at complementary rates. It was the Lord's good pleasure to bring us to know Him within two weeks of each other. The following week we attended a church that just happened to be initiating a home Bible study program, and we signed up for a new study. For the first year or so, there were only five in the study—Gayle, Noah, Ken, and the two of us. We started with the very basics as we journeyed through the Navigators' series of Bible studies.

Week after week after week, we plugged away discovering spiritual truth. It was the single most important factor in our early spiritual maturity. And it was the environment needed for us to hear and respond to God's calling us into full-time Christian service.

READ THROUGH THE BIBLE IN A YEAR TOGETHER

One of the great joys of Bible reading is that no matter where your level of spiritual understanding might be, there is always something in the text for you. You can be a brand new Christian and your mate can be an expert in theology, yet you both can discover something fresh and new. The deep resources of the Bible are sufficient to nourish every spiritual appetite.

Here are some helps that work for us:

Find a translation that fits both of you. Several excellent translations of the Bible are available. Besides the classic King James Version, you might consider the New American Standard Version, or the New International Version, just to name a couple.

Read from a good study Bible. There are a number of excellent study Bibles available, such as *The Ryrie Study Bible* (Chicago: Moody Press). The notes at the bottom of the pages, and the studies, maps, and concordance in the back can help you understand better what you read. Ask your pastor for some advice in this matter.

Find a printed "Read Through the Bible in a Year" schedule such as the American Bible Society provides. You'll have a guide for reading certain chapters each day of the year. That way you will always know what is required of you and what parts of the Bible you have already covered. Christian magazines, bookstores, and organizations often have yearly study guides, too. Many of the good study Bibles, like the one mentioned above, contain guides printed right inside the cover of the Bible. We find that handy, since there's no chance of misplacing it.

Try not to miss any days of reading. Force yourselves to plug away consistently, even though that might mean some days of reading while you are on the road, reading while you are waiting for an appointment, or even reading separately.

Pray for God's leading and the Holy Spirit's help before you begin to read. And pray for God's application of the spiritual truth after you have read.

Read out loud, so that you read at the same pace and are dealing with the same texts. Take turns reading (even if one of you is a better reader than the other).

Jot down questions for further study. If important spiritual questions come up about the text that neither of you has answers for, jot them down and ask your pastor for some help next time you have a chance.

Make it your goal to read through the Bible in a year. If you have it as a goal to read through the entire Bible in a year, every year, you'll have a standard against which to measure your progress, and you will ensure that you aren't slighting some portions of the Scripture at the expense of others.

READ A CHRISTIAN BOOK TOGETHER

Many excellent books are available that offer particular help in various areas of growth and problem solving. You will find yourself remembering and applying their truth much more faithfully if you read and discuss them together. Your pastor and your Christian friends can probably offer you a number of good suggestions. Remember, you won't both get the same things from each book, but good books will cause your spiritual lives to grow. Here are some books we recommend:

- *Knowing God*, by J. I. Packer (Downers Grove, Ill.: InterVarsity). Classic studies in the nature of God and His work in our lives and in this world. Without doubt, the single most important book next to the Bible in the spiritual growth of Steve and Janet Bly.
- *Mere Christianity*, by C. S. Lewis (New York: Macmillan). A powerful collection of essays covering subjects ranging from sexual morality to finding the meaning of the universe. Lewis provides intellectual support for many of our basic beliefs.
- *On Christian Truth*, by Harry Blamires (Ann Arbor, Mich.: Servant). A faith-building book in which the author persuasively examines the contents of the Christian faith. Blamires has a passion to teach us truly to think like Christians. This isn't pulp; it's hard-nosed Christianity.
- *Basic Christianity*, by John R. W. Stott (Downers Grove, Ill.: InterVarsity). A crystal-clear presentation of the basics of becoming and remaining a Christian. It will provide you with much ammunition in your role as a witness for Christ.
- *Spiritual Leadership*, by J. Oswald Sanders (Chicago: Moody). This book will be especially helpful for couples who see themselves together in leadership positions within the church. Sanders challenges us to excellence in our service to the Lord.
- *Loving God*, by Charles Colson (Grand Rapids, Mich.: Zondervan). An exhortation to be willing to pay the high cost of living out our faith in a hostile world, demonstrating as we do the characteristics of personal obedience and holiness.

FIND A CHRISTIAN MINISTRY THAT REQUIRES BOTH OF YOU

There are times for "his" and "her" church work. But it is equally important to discover a ministry that you can accomplish together. It might take you some time to discover such a ministry, but you will find it extremely rewarding to participate in a task in which both of you can exercise your distinctive gifts, talents, and ministries.

Steve's greatest teaching delight is to work with college-age students. Janet feels uncomfortable trying to teach such a group, but she enjoys getting to know them personally. Also, she feels relaxed about having a big gang in our home. So for many years we hosted a college-age potluck and Bible study group at our home. Janet's gifts of hospitality and mercy blended with Steve's gifts of teaching and exhortation. It was a rewarding ministry for both of us.

But when it comes to third graders, the roles reverse. Janet moves into the teacher's position, and Steve is in charge of recreation. Again, the gifts complement each other.

How can the two of you find such positions? List the three ministry areas that you personally feel best suited to accomplish at this time. Have your mate do the same. Then, working from these lists, start your search for work you can do for the Lord that allows each of you to use one of his high priority ministry gifts.

INSIST ON ATTENDING WORSHIP TOGETHER

If you are new Christians, or if you have stayed away from church for a while, it may be difficult for you to attend worship services together. Your ideal schedule may not include dressing up on Sunday mornings and going to town in order to sit still on a hard wooden bench. But a unified commitment by both husband and wife will break the unhealthy tendency to neglect public worship.

Worship with the community of fellow believers is not meant to be merely an option. Hebrews 10:25 reminds us that we should not "[forsake] our own assembling together."

However, lots of busy "church" folks never worship together either. He goes to the early service; she goes to the late. She worships in the morning; he in the evening. He's an usher; she always works in the baby nursery. She sings in the choir; he sits in the balcony.

Now that may be necessary. Certain ministries must take place during the worship service. But aim to have some times when you sit side by side for worship.

If the morning service separates you, make sure an evening service doesn't. Work hard to find a way. It is a mutually maturing and growing experience to place yourselves under the same worship leader and in the same worship service.

Become fanatically insistent on worship. It is extremely important to your spiritual life and growth. Go to worship together whether you are on vacation, on a business trip, or on a visit to the relatives. Be there when it's snowing, when it's raining, and when your brother-in-law pops by with his family for a Sunday morning visit.

TAKE TIME AFTER EVERY SERMON TO DISCUSS ITS CONTENTS WITH YOUR MATE

Nearly every sermon deserves ten to fifteen minutes of discussion. Some require ten to fifteen days. If you have to commute home, make the drive a time to discuss the sermon. If you have a big meal for lunch, use the "after-we-eat-and-before-we-do-the-dishes" time for a discussion of the main points.

Here are some ideas to make that time more meaningful:

- Reread the sermon text out loud.
- Review the sermon outline together, if one was provided.
- Take notes during the sermon for follow-up discussion.
- Discuss the ways the sermon should change your way of thinking or acting. Determine to put one specific suggestion into practice during the next week.
- Ask your mate to share how he thinks the message should affect *your* life.
- Talk about side benefits from the message. As you listened to the sermon, the Lord might have led you to some helpful spiritual thoughts that the preacher didn't cover. One verse, or illustration, or point of the sermon might have brought to mind another truth. Make sure your mate hears these additional thoughts as well.

Remember: The Lord can speak through the preached word to couples, to whole families, and to individuals. Don't overlook the message to the family unit.

FIND A HIDEAWAY WHERE THE TWO OF YOU CAN BE ALONE

Mates who are striving to be the best of friends need long, private talks. Christian mates need time for plenty of spiritual discussion if they are going to keep growing together in the Lord. Your own house doesn't normally work very well for that. The kids interrupt. The television interrupts. The telephone interrupts. Salesmen interrupt. Neighbors interrupt. Relatives interrupt. And even if you could miraculously prevent those intrusions, all those jobs staring at you around the house will nag you to "stop goofing off and get to work!"

Your hideaway should not be farther than about a half-hour away from home (ten minutes or less is ideal), and ideally it should be free of expense—anything else might put restrictions on how often you slip away.

If you live in San Diego, West Palm Beach, South Padre Island, or Lahaina, Maui, you can just pick a park bench down the street almost any time of the year. The rest of us experience seasonal weather prohibitions.

Maybe for you two it's a back booth in a little Italian cafe in a neighboring city where no one knows your name. One of the best retreats can be a walk, hand in hand, far away from the sounds of home.

Such time together is not a luxury but a necessity, especially if your regular life-style is a hectic, frantic push. It will give you time to discuss what's really happening in your private spiritual lives. Don't wait for an explosion six months from now to discuss a situation that is boiling in your spirit today.

ATTEND AT LEAST ONE COUPLES' SEMINAR A YEAR

The seminar can be a week-long summer conference in the woods. It can be a special weekend retreat at a convention center in a neighboring city. It might be a Saturday seminar at your home church. Every couple interested in continual spiritual growth will need input of new ideas and challenges. You will also want to have times to visit with other couples who are struggling with some of the same things you are.

If you don't know where such conferences are held, ask your pastor for a recommendation. Check with your denomination for upcoming marriage and family conferences. Quiz your Christian friends, both in your church and in other churches, as to the seminars they attend. Watch the church page in your local newspaper for information about what is happening in your own town. Often Christian bookstores display flyers about such events.

If finances absolutely prevent you from attending one of these seminars, check with the organizers. Often there is scholarship money available. Don't hesitate to take it if you are truly in need. That's exactly why the money was given. Check with your pastor or church board to see if the church might be able to help financially.

Look for a seminar to attend that you can both agree upon. You will not achieve the desired result if one of you must be dragged kicking and screaming to a given conference or seminar. But be sensitive to each other. A particular seminar might not be something that is of high interest to you, yet it could be just what your mate needs.

BE DILIGENT IN HAVING A REGULAR PRAYER TIME TOGETHER

Don't wait until summer or winter, the baby's born, or the baby's grown. Don't wait until you build your house or sell your house, you finish night school or finish the night shift. Start a regular prayer time together right now because it never, ever gets easier.

Some guidelines:

- Both the husband and the wife should pray.
- There should be no competition (who can pray the longest or the loudest; whose prayers are the most theologically astute).
- There should be prayer for family members, for each other, and for God's work in the world. Specific prayers for your children should be a part of every day's petitions. (In *How to Be a Good Mom* (Chicago: Moody, p. 57), we share a comprehensive guide to praying for your children.)
- There should be prayers of heartfelt praise and thanksgiving.

It's surprising how many couples today are convinced that they need some further encouragement in building their marriage and yet never consider strengthening their spiritual lives together. Perhaps some of us pastors and wives are the most guilty. We can cram a week, a month, or a year with spiritual activity in our own separate realms, but we ignore our spiritual growth together as husband and wife.

Best friends just won't let that sort of thing happen.

9

When Bad Things Happen

As if she didn't have enough to go through . . .

After years and years of wealth and luxury, now she had only the dress on her back.

A former reputation and status of being one of the country's leading ladies; now she roamed garbage dumps for a meal.

She used to have a large healthy family that was the pride of her life; now she was childless.

Her healthy, vibrant, dynamic husband had become a pitiful, broken-down, sore-infested old man. Let's face it, that's enough for any one gal to handle.

But on top of all that, her husband was a religious fanatic who sat around wondering what God was trying to tell him through all this. He would pop up with quotes like: "Naked I came from my mother's womb, and naked I shall return there. The Lord gave and the Lord has taken away. Blessed be the name of the Lord" (Job 1:21).

What do you do when bad things happen to your mate? Well, here's what Mrs. Job said: "Do you still hold fast your integrity? Curse God and die!" (Job 2:9).

Not exactly what we hope a good friend will say.

Why is it that bad things happen to people like us? And what should we do when bad things happen to our mate?

WHY DO BAD THINGS HAPPEN?

SOMETIMES BECAUSE OF DIVINE APPOINTMENT

That was certainly the case for Job. The Bible tells us that Satan had a conversation in heaven with God. "Then the Lord said to Satan, 'Behold, all that he has is in your power, only do not put forth your hand on him' " (Job 1:12). And when Satan wanted to do even more to Job, "the Lord said to Satan, 'Behold, he is in your power, only spare his life' " (Job 2:6).

Job was caught up in a cosmic spiritual conflict between God and Satan. No wonder he had such a difficult time understanding what was happening.

The conflict continues in our day.

"For our struggle is not against flesh and blood, but against the rulers, against the powers, against the world forces of this darkness, against the spiritual forces of wickedness in the heavenly places" (Ephesians 6:12).

Bad things continue to happen to us as the casualties of these spiritual battles spill over into our lives.

At times the divinely appointed circumstances that bring about the bad times are meant to teach us spiritual lessons. In Jonah 4:7 we learn that "God appointed a worm when dawn came the next day, and it attacked the plant and it withered." So Jonah's plant died. Big deal.

Well, it was to Jonah, for he had been sitting in the shade of the plant.

"And it came about when the sun came up that God appointed a scorching east wind, and the sun beat down on Jonah's head so that he became faint and begged with all his soul to die, saying, 'Death is better to me than life' " (Jonah 4:8).

God replied to Jonah, "You had compassion on the plant for which you did not work, and which you did not cause to grow, which came up overnight and perished overnight. And should I not have compassion on Nineveh, the great city in which there are more than 120,000 persons who do not know the difference between their right and left hand, as well as many animals? (4:10-11)

Jonah didn't die, but he learned a lasting spiritual lesson.

Paul's powerful evangelistic ministry was threatened by a physical affliction. The apostle pleaded repeatedly with the Lord to relieve his pain. God had something else in mind:

> And because of the surpassing greatness of the revelations, for this reason, to keep me from exalting myself, there was given me a thorn in the flesh, a messenger of Satan to buffet me—to keep me from exalting myself! Concerning this I entreated the Lord three times that it might depart from me. And He has said to me, "My grace is sufficient for you, for power is perfected in weakness." (2 Corinthians 12:7-9)

God appointed a thorn in the flesh for Paul that actually helped God bring out the best in Paul's life and ministry.

There's a sense in which every bad time is an appointment by God, since He reigns in sovereignty over all things. But we can discover several more immediate causes for the bad times.

SOMETIMES BECAUSE OF NATURAL CATASTROPHE

The earth quakes. Volcanoes erupt. Waves pound. Fires jump creeks. Bridges collapse. Plagues surge across the land. We do not live in a perfect world.

However, it was perfect once. "And God saw all that He had made, and behold, it was very good" (Genesis 1:31).

We are the cause of the earth's present upheaval.

"Then to Adam He said, 'Because you have listened to the voice of your wife, and have eaten from the tree about which I commanded you, saying, "You shall not eat from it"; cursed is the ground because of you' " (Genesis 3:17).

But our planet will not stay in this condition forever.

"For the anxious longing of the creation waits eagerly for the revealing of the sons of God. For the creation was subjected to futility not of its own will, but because of Him who subjected it, in hope that the creation itself also will be set free from its slavery to corruption into the freedom of the glory of the children of God. For we know that the whole creation groans and suffers the pains of childbirth together until now" (Romans 8:19-22).

When that day comes, nature as we know it will be vastly changed.

112 Be Your Mate's Best Friend

"The mountains and the hills will break forth into shouts of joy before you, and all the trees of the field will clap their hands. Instead of the thorn bush the cypress will come up; and instead of the nettle the myrtle will come up; and it will be a memorial to the Lord, for an everlasting sign which will not be cut off" (Isaiah 55:12-13).

But that day hasn't come yet, so we look for explanations. The religious people in Jesus' day had a fairly simple explanation. If bad things happened, it was because of the victim's sin. They saw even natural disasters as merely God's punishing certain individuals.

Jesus wouldn't let them hold such a view of God. "Or do you suppose that those eighteen on whom the tower in Siloam fell and killed them, were worse culprits than all the men who live in Jerusalem? I tell you, no, but unless you repent, you will all likewise perish" (Luke 13:4-5).

Jesus made it clear that all have sinned. If God wanted to use natural disaster to eradicate sin, who would be left? Remember, He did that once, and only the eight on Noah's ark survived the Flood. Jesus implied that the tower fell because it was one of the tragedies that naturally occur in this sin-tainted world. Some bad times occur for no other reason than that.

SOMETIMES BECAUSE OF WORLDLY TRIBULATION

The tenor of society, the flow of civilization, and the dominating ideas of our worldly system oppose God's plan for His people. The collision of these three forces produces tragic times.

Jesus said, "These things I have spoken to you, that in Me you may have peace. In the world you have tribulation, but take courage; I have overcome the world" (John 16:33).

The armed forces of Babylon marched against Jerusalem and defeated it. Then they carried off the people, both the faithful and the apostate, to a country far away. One of the survivors wrote, "By the rivers of Babylon, there we sat down and wept, when we remembered Zion. Upon the willows in the midst of it we hung our harps. For there our captors demanded of us sons, and our tormentors mirth, saying, 'Sing us one of the songs of Zion.' How can we sing the Lord's song in a foreign land?" (Psalm 137:1-4)

Make a stand for good! March to support a biblical position! Protest for what is right! Demand justice and mercy! You'll always find fervent, sometimes vicious, opponents. In this world there is tribulation.

SOMETIMES BECAUSE OF OUR OWN FOOLISHNESS

Hezekiah deserves high marks as a king of Judah. In the company of numerous ungodly tyrants, he stands out.

"And thus Hezekiah did throughout all Judah; and he did what was good, right, and true before the Lord his God. And every work which he began in the service of the house of God in law and in commandment, seeking his God, he did with all his heart and prospered" (2 Chronicles 31:20-21).

But even Hezekiah was not above foolishness. One thoughtless act proved costly to the whole country. The episode is recorded in Isaiah 38 and 39.

Deathly ill, the king pleads to the Lord for his life. God grants him fifteen more years. Soon after his recovery a contingent of officials from the not yet powerful country of Babylon arrives to express their congratulations upon his recovery. Hezekiah thrives on all the attention and proudly shows them just how important and wealthy he really is. He gives his guests a royal tour of the riches of the kingdom, including the vaults of gold, silver, and jewels.

The prophet Isaiah was incensed. "Hear the word of the Lord of hosts, 'Behold, the days are coming when all that is in your house, and all that your fathers have laid up in store to this day shall be carried to Babylon; nothing shall be left,' says the Lord" (Isaiah 39:6).

Hezekiah shrugged off the prophet's talk of doom. "Oh, well, at least it won't happen during my lifetime."

A future generation suffered the devastation of the Babylonian plunder caused by Hezekiah's lack of discretion and wisdom.

SOMETIMES BECAUSE PEOPLE GIVE SATAN ENTRY

There's no question that Judas faced bad times. After betraying Jesus, he began to have second thoughts. He even tried to reverse the consequence of his sin, or at least appease his guilty conscience.

"Then when Judas, who had betrayed Him, saw that He had been condemned, he felt remorse and returned the thirty pieces of silver to the chief priests and elders, saying, 'I have sinned by betraying innocent blood' " (Matthew 27:3-4).

But he found no relief from his guilt. "And he went away and hanged himself" (Matthew 27:5).

How did a disciple of Jesus come to such a shocking end? The Scriptures give the answer: "And Satan entered into Judas who was called Iscariot, belonging to the number of the twelve. And he went away and discussed with the chief priests and officers how he might betray Him to them. And they were glad, and agreed to give him money" (Luke 22:3-5).

Greed so controlled Judas's life that he actually gave Satan direct control. John confirms this: "Now he [Judas] said this, not because he was concerned about the poor, but because he was a thief, and as he had the money box, he used to pilfer what was put into it" (John 12:6).

The lust for more begins with a small temptation. Just a few dollars or coins missing. A wink, a casual touch, or a pornographic film. It can start there, but it won't stop there. Private desire, unchecked, can lead to addiction, and surrender of the will to Satan's control.

SOMETIMES BECAUSE OF OUR OWN PERSONAL SIN

Satan does not have to possess us in order for our sinful actions to mess up our lives. The logical consequences of our disobedience to God bring many tough times. Jesus' followers were wrong to think that all tribulations are due to personal sin, but certainly some of them are.

There was a man near the pool of Bethesda, in Jerusalem, who had had a crippling disease for thirty-eight years. Jesus healed him miraculously, then presented him with a challenge: "Behold, you have become well; do not sin anymore, so that nothing worse may befall you" (John 5:14).

Sin has its consequences.

Paul warned Christians: "Do not be deceived, God is not mocked; for whatever a man sows, this he will also reap" (Galatians 6:7).

An alcoholic ruins his liver.

A prostitute acquires venereal disease.

A habitual gambler faces bankruptcy.

There are some bad times to be endured that need no further explanation than the statement, "I have sinned."

SOMETIMES BECAUSE OF OUR WITNESS FOR CHRIST

Peter and John were hauled before the supreme religious court of the land three times. Their crime? The high priest spelled it out: "We gave you strict orders not to continue teaching in this name, and behold, you have filled Jerusalem with your teaching, and intend to bring this man's blood upon us" (Acts 5:28).

They were arrested for telling people about Jesus Christ.

But some folks thought that simple arrest was letting them get off pretty easily. A further punishment was added: "They flogged them and ordered them to speak no more in the name of Jesus, and then released them" (Acts 5:40).

Peter and John were beaten raw with a lead-embedded leather whip before they were allowed to go home. That kind of treatment surely didn't stop those two. "And every day, in the temple and from house to house, they kept right on teaching and preaching Jesus as the Christ" (Acts 5:42).

Making a public stand for Jesus did not make their life easier. It never does. But they weren't about to stop their preaching just because the bad times rolled.

Bad times come our way.

That's the only kind of world—the only kind of life—we have available.

It is often difficult to understand exactly why we are facing trials and tribulations. It is often impossible to know why others, especially loved ones, are up against hard times. Yet the important question is not necessarily *"Why* is this happening?" but rather, *"What* should we do now?"

Eight Things You Can Do
When Your Mate Is Facing Bad Times

STAND BY YOUR MATE

"There is a friend who sticks closer than a brother" (Proverbs 18:24). That's the kind of friend your mate needs when he's up against tough trials. Bad times can make introverts out of outgoing personalities. All of a sudden, they want to be alone and don't want to go anywhere. If there is personal failure (moral, financial, social) they won't want to talk about it.

Mates often react the same way. It's easy to let in a flood of resentment. "I'm not the one who messed things up, but now I have to live with it." "It was all your fault; you go explain it to the neighbors!"

More than ever, your mate needs someone on his side. Even if the difficulty was brought on by his foolish actions, you can demonstrate forgiveness and faithful love, without agreeing with everything he did. If at all possible, don't let him go anywhere without you. This is the "worse" that you agreed to when you pledged at the altar, "for better or worse." You now have a striking opportunity to demonstrate that commitment in a practical way.

PROVE YOURSELF TO BE A KIND LISTENER

Remember Mrs. Job? She'd have been better off not to say anything at all. In fact, Job's so-called friends had the same problem.

At first, they came to "sympathize with him and comfort him" (Job 2:11). But when they saw his loss, his sorrow, and his pain they sat speechless for seven days. That's when Job got up the courage to tell them what he was thinking. What he needed—and what he thought he had—were some friends who cared enough to just listen as he rambled on about his grief. But instead, they quickly jumped to the offense. "Job, we know exactly why this happened to you, you old sinner."

James' advice fits in at this point. "But let everyone be quick to hear, slow to speak, and slow to anger" (James 1:19).

There is a time to talk and a time to listen. When the weight of your mate's bad times are about to crush him, just listen. Listen with your ears, your heart, and your mind. Grasp all he says, all he implies, all that lies hidden within. Plan on long lunches, late nights, early mornings. Turn off the TV, put down the book, cancel the golf game, and give him all your attention.

CONTINUE TO SHOW YOUR SPOUSE LOVE

"A friend loves at all times" (Proverbs 17:17). When you are your mate's best friend you love him even when he's failed. You demonstrate your love to him no matter how enormous the difficulty ahead of him might be.

In times like this your mate needs love that he understands. The neighbors think they know all about your problem, but you meet your spouse in the driveway with an open hug and big kiss.

Think of those loving actions that will impress your mate most. Cancel other activities, because "he needs me, you know." "I've got to help her work through this."

SEEK GOD'S COUNSEL TOGETHER

"And as for you, you meant evil against me, but God meant it for good" (Genesis 50:20). The Lord majors in thwarting evil by accomplishing His ultimate purposes anyway. No matter what the cause, no matter how serious the failure, He's able to turn it around. But you'll never discover God's purpose unless you seek His help and guidance.

If your mate is too overwhelmed by the bad time, sit, stand, or kneel alongside him and do the praying.

Remember the paralytic man in Mark 2 whose friends let him down through the roof right above Jesus' head? That man was not only healed, but his sins were forgiven. But on his own he was in no shape to do anything. He needed someone to carry him into the Lord's presence.

When your mate is going through tough times, he might need to be mentally and spiritually carried into the presence of Almighty God. If he is unable or unwilling to pray, seek God's will, or read God's Word, do it with him anyway. Don't let him imagine even for a day that he can survive those tough times without the help of God.

HELP YOUR MATE ACCEPT RESPONSIBILITY

"Faithful are the wounds of a friend" (Proverbs 27:6). Show him beyond a doubt that you're on his side; then allow him, when he's ready, to admit personal failure.

At times, friends must provide correction. That can hurt. But it's like the pain of the antiseptic in an injury. After the pain comes quick healing.

But effective correction requires special sensitivity: "Restore such a one in a spirit of gentleness; each one looking to yourself, lest you too be tempted" (Galatians 6:1).

Sometimes a circumstance is so unbearable that it may require weeks, months, or years to confess the whole story. Allow your mate to work at his own pace, but don't allow him off the hook.

Private sins can be confessed in private. Public sins should be confessed in public. Help him to come to that point so that total spiritual healing can take place.

Remember—not all bad times come because of sin. But when they do, help him face up to his personal responsibility in the matter.

REVIEW GOD'S FAITHFULNESS

Remind your mate of God's faithfulness, provisions, and blessings in the past. Not all the times have been this bad. There were good times—days and years. Some things have gone right. There are loving memories, wonderful surprises, and special events to relive. Bad times often narrow our vision. We can only see the slice of life that we are now experiencing. Best friends can review the whole picture.

The writer of Psalm 73 suffered this same temporary shortsightedness. He was plodding through difficulties, while the ungodly all around him seemed to be taking life easy. "Unfair!" he cried.

"When I pondered to understand this, it was troublesome in my sight until I came into the sanctuary of God; then I perceived their end" (vv. 16-17). When he finally grasped the long-range view of life, his heart and mind quieted in understanding.

As your mate's best friend, help him remember that the same God who provided the blessings in the past can be counted on even now.

CHART NEW GOALS AND DREAMS TOGETHER

This unexpected situation may have crushed certain plans you had made. The severely injured leg means she will never play tennis again. Getting fired from the job means he'll never be the executive vice-president. The devastating loss of income means you will never have the house on the hill.

But no matter how crucial the earlier plans seemed, there are other goals and dreams to follow. Even spiritually motivated projects are sometimes taken away from us, and we must look for new opportunities.

Acts 16:6-10 tells how Paul tried repeatedly to enter the northern region of Asia Minor. God prevented him. Paul had left his home church in Antioch telling them all about the frontier ministry he planned to start in Bithynia. But he couldn't even get past the country's border.

Paul and his companions didn't stay depressed for long. Suddenly, a new direction was placed in front of them. "Come over to Macedonia and help us," the man in the vision said, and off they went. The failure of one dream led to an opportunity for another.

HELP YOUR MATE ALLOW GOD TIME TO WORK HIS BEST

One thing we can all agree upon concerning bad times: we want them to end in a hurry. "If there is a lesson to learn in all this," we say, "I want to learn it fast!" But some things are not learned quickly.

Paul suffered a "thorn in the flesh" (2 Corinthians 12:7). Eventually he realized that God meant him to learn that "My grace is sufficient for you, for power is perfected in weakness" (v. 9). But that insight came only after much pleading, praying, and questioning on Paul's part. It's a tough lesson for someone who is in constant pain.

Even new Christians have had Romans 8:28 tossed at them: "And we know that God causes all things to work together for good to those who love God, to those who are called according to His purpose." But those words can seem unreal and remote when your world has just crashed in on you.

As a mate, you have time on your side. Your pledge before God was to be with this person until death. You don't need to grab for an easy, quick-fix solution or explanation for your mate's tough times.

Our friend Rod owned a nice little western wear store a few miles down the road from the city. It was more or less a "mom and pop" operation, with a couple of longtime employees. Then Rod got a chance to move up to the big time. A huge shopping center was going in downtown in the high rent district. A businessman whom Rod had known for years wanted him to become a partner in an ambitious new store in the mall.

Rod jumped at the chance. After all, the kids were in high school, and there would soon be college bills, weddings, and all that. After several delays, and countless trips to the bankers, attorneys, and accountants, they signed a wagonload of documents.

After a rush of sales the first two weeks, the business began to flounder. Rod soon ran out of clientele interested in wearing boots and cowboy hats. But the daily stress of overhead and inventory costs remained. Rod wasn't used to this kind of pressure.

But his partner continued to wheel and deal. He secured another sizable loan from the bank and assured Rod that the Christmas season would get them in the black.

It didn't.

On December 29, Rod's partner decided he would rather live in the South Pacific supported by most of the bank loan.

By February 1 the new store had folded, and by March 1 Rod's original store and his spacious five-bedroom ranch house were taken over by the lending institution.

Rod was devastated. He blamed himself. "I was too greedy for gain to investigate this guy more," he admitted.

Now Rod, Nancy, and the kids live in an apartment next to the city park. He works as a clerk for a hardware store. Nancy keeps books for an insurance company. If their oldest finds a part-time job, he can go to a community junior college in September.

But there remains a glowing inspiration in all of this to those of us who have watched them from a distance. His wife, Nancy, lets everyone know she still thinks Rod is the greatest guy on earth. She initiates social times with their friends. She tags along with him as they bounce from attorneys to courtrooms to criminal investigations. She is by his side at basketball games, church meetings, and at the supermarket.

Not once has anyone heard her complain about having to give up the house or the business and start over.

Rod may have lost nearly everything else in the world, but he still has his best friend.

10

Keep On Forgiving

She was definitely not the type you would take home to Mamma. Let's face it, she wasn't merely a little wild; she was a professional.

Now, he was a nice enough guy. Overly religious, some would say. But, it was her chance to get her life straightened out. With a husband who loved her and three children, she found respect in society at last.

But it wasn't long until she slipped back into the habits of the past. She ran off with some guy and deserted the husband and kids. Soon she was back in business, selling her sexual favors.

If he had listened to his friends and relatives he would have said "good riddance" and dumped her. Surely someone told him, "Settle down, raise the kids, and find yourself a good woman this time." Well, if he received such advice, he rejected it. He was driven by a higher guidance. He went after her, brought her back home, restored her to her previous status, and, most of all, forgave her.

It might have all the zing of a soap opera, but it's straight from Scripture. The man was Hosea, the prophet. The woman, his wife, Gomer. You can find the account in Hosea, chapters 1–3.

The divine lesson of the book of Hosea is that God is willing and ready to forgive us, if we will only turn from our idolatrous ways. To exemplify this truth the Bible provides a classic example of forgiving a mate.

Every marriage needs forgiveness. It's an inescapable part of human relationships. Yet some folks remain deceived. They fall for the old "Perfect Mate" theory. You know, the idea that out there somewhere is a Perfect Mate; and when I find him and we get married, everything will be just as I always dreamed it would be.

But two weeks, or two years, or twenty years later you wake up one morning and realize that everything in your married life is not perfect; so you decide that you must have picked the wrong mate. If that feeling is left unchecked it can lead to your dumping the mate and continuing the search for perfection.

It's a dumb theory.

There are no perfect people. None. Anywhere. Ever.

"For all have sinned and fall short of the glory of God" (Romans 3:23).

"If we say that we have no sin, we are deceiving ourselves, and the truth is not in us" (1 John 1:8).

Thus, every mate on the face of this earth will make some mistakes. Some of those mistakes will be more serious than others, and some will be very difficult to forgive.

Deborah left Gavin and the four girls and ran off to Denver with an insurance salesman. Six months later Deborah showed up on Gavin's doorstep asking to be forgiven. He's finding it very difficult to accept her back.

Hugh had been the bookkeeper at Mid-Valley Steel for over seventeen years. Then someone discovered fifty-two thousand dollars missing—and Hugh had a history of Las Vegas trips. He was fired from his job; criminal investigations were pending. It was splashed across the paper nearly every week. Carole just couldn't take it. She and the kids moved to Sacramento, but Hugh keeps hoping that she will forgive.

It's been a difficult marriage. Howard and Barbara were barely eighteen. They had a lot of growing up to do. It's seven years later and immaturity still shows. When Barbara's younger sister, Elaine, finally told her that Howard had made a pass at her shortly after their marriage, it was all she could stand. She hasn't left him, but he sleeps on the couch at night. Forgiveness is not in sight.

On and on the accounts go. Some acts are horrible, vicious, and cruel. Some are subtle, persistent, deceptive. They range from wife beating to continual public ridicule, until the mate has had enough. A mental line is drawn. She says to herself "I've had it," and refuses to forgive.

Fortunately not every marriage has to face the severe dilemmas mentioned above, but every marriage has difficult trials that only true forgiveness can solve. Some marriages are so crammed with a lack of forgiveness for minor things that the whole relationship is in jeopardy. That was the case with Pauline and Darrin.

Pauline rushed into Steve's office. She said she was thinking about leaving Darrin. Then she rattled off a list of things that had pushed her to that point. He was a half-hour late to Mikki's school program. It had been three years and he still hadn't finished painting the garage. He went fishing again last Sunday when he promised not to. He won't be nice to her brother. He insists on wearing that horrible, old, green sweater. He cancelled her subscription to a soap opera magazine. He buys a six pack of beer every weekend. And he refuses to let her cut her hair.

Every marriage needs lots of forgiveness. There is no way to be your mate's best friend unless you learn how to let forgiveness dominate your daily relationship.

Why Is Forgiveness So Difficult?

BECAUSE WE ARE SELFISH PEOPLE

Let's be honest about it. Our world centers around our own personal needs, wants, and dreams. In marriage we attempt to break out of that narrowness and allow another human into our circle. But it's difficult. Even as Christians we have to fight against our old way of responding and our old nature that looks out for "me first."

"I thought I had proper justification for my anger. Look, we've been married over twenty-five years and Janet still hasn't changed. You see, I like cold cereal for breakfast. My day doesn't begin without a big bowl of Cheerios. But it is extremely important to have very cold milk on the cereal. Lukewarm milk won't do. All I ask is that she put the milk bottle back into the refrigerator immediately after she uses it so that the milk will remain very cold for my cereal. Now that's not too much to expect, right? So why, after all these years, is the milk still left on the counter? After 9,396 days of marriage do I still have to forgive?"

Yep.

When our selfishness is the cause of our own hurt, we have no choice but to forgive quickly. But sometimes the source of the difficulty is much deeper than that.

BECAUSE SOMETHING PRECIOUS HAS BEEN TAKEN FROM US

"I just can't trust him anymore. He said he wouldn't stop by the bar anymore. He said he would bring his paycheck straight home. He said he wouldn't drive drunk. He said he wouldn't embarrass me in front of the neighbors. I love him, God knows I love him, but I can't count on his keeping his word. I just can't trust him. He tells me it's going to be different, but I've heard that too many times before."

You've heard a similar tirade. Maybe you have been the one to speak it. Trust is a precious commodity. Our world seems to be pushing toward a complete lack of trust of everyone. We don't trust the government, the courts, or our neighbors. We have to have long written contracts at every step in life and then we don't trust the contracts.

It is a delight to get married and find a mate whom you can trust. You have the freedom to be yourself and not worry about maintaining some illusionary image. Your mate will not tell the world what you look like without makeup. Your mate will not discuss your lack of experience in making love. Your mate will not steal your golf money to buy booze. Your mate will not tell your inner secrets to the next door neighbors. Your mate can be counted on to keep his word.

Then something happens. It can be something big. It can be an accumulation of little things. All of a sudden you realize the trust you once had is gone. Now he has become like all the others. Now you are on your own again. There is no one to trust. That one vital element of a stable relationship has been stolen, and you are not sure if you will ever be able to find it again.

The road to restoring trust is long and difficult. If a mate is truthful when he says, "I just can't trust you anymore," make sure you understand the seriousness of the problem. It will take more than a quick, "I'm sorry," and an "I forgive you" to fully restore the relationship.

Sometimes the difficulty of forgiveness is based not merely on the mental struggle of regaining trust but on the damage done to a spiritual union. Marriage is more than a legal, social, emotional, mental, and physical relationship.

"What therefore God has joined together, let no man separate" is not a sweet sentiment used at weddings by preachers. Those words were spoken by Jesus Christ. He expects us to honor them (Matthew 19:6).

Why is this point so critically important? It is important because of the unity created by the marriage. In the same verse Christ stated, "They are no longer two, but one flesh."

To destroy that oneness is to rip apart something God has made. That is why adultery, which destroys oneness, should be so unthinkable.

But sexual unfaithfulness does take place. Those deep, spiritual bonds are broken. Forgiveness is extremely difficult but not, as Hosea's example reminds us, impossible.

WHY MUST WE PRESS ON TO FORGIVE?

WE MUST FORGIVE FOR THE OFFENDER'S SAKE

We all deserve another chance. If we only had one chance at all of life's opportunities, we would never succeed at anything. Few things that are worthwhile are completely mastered at the first attempt. We don't lift a twelve-month infant to his feet and demand, "From now on you have to walk!" We don't buy little Sissy a piano and then hand her a complicated concerto and say, "If you play one note wrong we are taking the piano away."

Years of building poor habits, years of self-centered behavior, years of having little self-control are not reversed instantly by wedding vows. Every marriage relationship must have some room for the relationship to grow, change, mature. We have an opportunity to teach our mate something about the Lord's forgiveness by an open demonstration of our own.

Our mates have no excuse for sin. They have no reasonable explanation for rebellion against God or against His Word (besides the fact that we are all sinners). But that does not place them beyond our scope of forgiveness. They need someone who will hang in there with them even when the imperfections are obvious.

WE MUST FORGIVE FOR OUR OWN SAKE

When we choose not to forgive, we multiply our own sorrows. Not forgiving robs us of our full potential. It alters how we look at every action and every event. It dominates our decisions. We become slaves to it, and it affects our spirit, our minds, and our bodies. Our lives are difficult enough without the burden of unforgiven relationships.

Hebrews 12:15 warns us to see to it that "no root of bitterness springing up causes us trouble." When we withhold forgiveness, we multiply bitterness. It costs something to be bitter. Lack of forgiveness between marriage partners turns God-intended pleasure into a battlefield where everyone is on the losing side.

Deanna turned into a compulsive shopper sometime after her third child was born. Ross had to battle with her to keep her within the family budget. By taking an extra job he finally paid off the charge accounts. He thought he was making some progress. She attended some counseling. She knew she had a problem. They developed a system whereby she hardly ever shopped without taking Ross along. But last fall she discovered television shopping. She could sit at home and pick out what she wanted. When a company sent a guaranteed acceptance credit card application in her name, she gave in and sent for the card.

Before Ross caught on, he had a $3,000 charge account to pay off. Well, Deanna's truly sorry. She offered to get a job and pay off the account herself. She knows she is going to need continuing help. But Ross isn't taking any chances. He has put the bank accounts in his name, has destroyed all the credit cards, has found a way to lock out the home shopping channel, and has told the businesses around town not to let Deanna buy anything.

Ask Ross and he would say he has the problem under control. But he sounds puzzled when he admits that Deanna just doesn't seem very affectionate anymore. Relationships between warden and inmate are never very warm. True forgiveness would find a practical way for Deanna gradually to reestablish her credibility and regain Ross's trust.

It's serious business not to forgive others. Lack of forgiveness means we restrict God's forgiveness for us. "For if you forgive men for their transgressions, your heavenly Father will also forgive you. But if you do not forgive men, then your Father will not forgive your transgressions" (Matthew 6:14-15).

Stephen understood this principle in Acts 7:60. After seeing Jesus in heaven, Stephen's last breath was a prayer for those who were killing him: "Lord, do not hold this sin against them!"

Face to face with the Lord, you are going to want all the forgiveness available to you. There is no time for an unforgiving heart.

WE MUST FORGIVE FOR THE GOSPEL'S SAKE

If for no other reason, forgiveness is needed because forgiveness is commanded. Paul writes in Ephesians 4:32, "And be kind to one another, tender-hearted, forgiving each other, just as God in Christ also has forgiven you."

If Paul felt the necessity of such a command, that indicates that he recognized that Christians would, indeed, slip back into sin and do things that needed forgiving. He also knew that forgiveness was not an automatic reaction among believers—for why would he have had reason to command something that would happen automatically?

It is our duty as believers to follow the Scriptures, which in their entirety are "inspired by God and profitable for teaching, for reproof, for correction, for training in righteousness" (2 Timothy 3:16). Sometimes the force of duty to obey helps us forgive.

WE MUST FORGIVE FOR OUR WITNESS'S SAKE

We have all tried to share our faith with someone who countered our remarks with the observation, "Well, I once knew a Christian who. . . ." Then he relates a horrible example of a brother or sister in the faith who had his or her life so messed up that it repelled rather than attracted outsiders.

How in the world are you going to get those non-Christian neighbors to go to church with you if you and your mate are no longer speaking to each other? Wouldn't that be a great witnessing tool?

"Well, my husband is a louse. After twelve years of marriage I just found out he gets paid twice a month, not once a month. I'm so mad I haven't spoken to him in three days. . . . By the way, it's "Invite a Friend Day" at our church and we would like you to be our guests. We can give you a ride, provided you don't mind sitting in the back seat with that no-good husband of mine." Really tempting, right?

WE MUST FORGIVE FOR OTHER PEOPLE'S SAKE

When husband and wife refuse to forgive each other, they force all their relatives and friends to take sides. They want to support both, but the couple has removed that option. Even the kids don't know what is going on. When they notice Daddy sleeping on the couch every night, they want to know why. They want to know if they should be mad at him or at Mom.

If your mate has done something wrong and the whole community knows, people are looking at you to see your reaction. If you are able to forgive, then they know it's all right for them to forgive as well. If you aren't able to do so, the children, the neighbors, and the co-workers are forced to alienate themselves from one of the combatants. Forgiveness could eliminate that increasing complication.

Here are four facts to remember about forgiveness:

Fact 1. Complete forgiveness most often requires confession and repentance. In teaching on forgiveness, Jesus said, "If he sins against you seven times a day, and returns to you seven times, saying, 'I repent,' forgive him" (Luke 17:4).

Forgiveness does not mean overlooking your mate's sinful actions. Your mate must be confronted with God's standards. (More about how to do that appears in chapter 12.)

It might take some time before your mate is ready to admit his mistake. Facing up to failures takes some time. We have to learn first how to admit to ourselves that we have flunked. Give your mate some time.

There are a few sins that are done in such ignorance that forgiveness can be granted even before the participant knows they have done something wrong. Jesus looked down at the Roman soldiers around the cross and prayed, "Father, forgive them; for they do not know what they are doing" (Luke 23:34). To our knowledge, the soldiers never confessed any sin, but forgiveness was offered nonetheless.

Suppose your mate tells an off-color joke at a party. In anger you stare at him—and realize he hasn't a clue as to what's bothering you. You don't have to wait until your mate comes confessing—you can forgive him instantly. That will allow you to talk to him later, not by confronting or condemning him, but in a spirit of encouragement and correction.

Fact 2. Some offenses need repeated forgiveness. Remember the strong words of Jesus in Luke 17:4. He told us that if anyone sins against us seven times in the same day and continues to seek forgiveness, we must forgive.

In Matthew 18:21-22, Peter asked if he had to forgive seven times, to which Jesus replied, "seventy times seven." That meant, of course, that we must always be forgiving and re-forgiving.

Forgiveness that says, "I'll forgive just this one time," or "This is the last time I'll forgive," isn't true forgiveness. Your mate might have a real struggle that will require a lifetime of forgiveness. Jesus wants us to be prepared to do just that.

Fact 3. Forgiveness begins in the heart. Jesus said, "So shall my heavenly Father also do to you, if each of you does not forgive his brother from your heart" (Matthew 18:35).

You are not kidding anyone, especially not the Lord, when you say, "I forgive you," and yet cling to resentment and bitterness. The best way to move the heart away from such a state is to fill it with thoughts and acts of love for the person you are trying to forgive.

You might not feel very loving at the moment toward a mate who has greatly offended you and now seeks forgiveness, but acts of love can help the heart change and replace unforgiveness with true forgiveness.

Fact 4. Forgiveness is extremely difficult, but it is worth the work. After the disciples had heard the hard lesson about forgiving over and over again, they said to the Lord, "Increase our faith!" (Luke 17:5) They could see clearly there was nothing easy about that kind of radical forgiveness.

But, of course, the end result is worth the effort. Forgiveness in marriage means you are serious about preserving the most important human friendship God has allowed you to have. Forgiveness is a public declaration to God and all witnesses that you are striving to live a life that reflects the image of your Lord and Savior, Jesus Christ. Forgiveness is an open demonstration that you follow a different path than the bitterness and revenge of this world.

How Can I Ever Forgive My Mate?

SEEK GOD'S HELP

You must have God's help. If you are having difficulty forgiving your mate, that must be the top priority of your prayer life. As you pray do the following:

- Ask God to reveal any sin in your own life that might have caused the offensive action in your mate.
- Ask God to reveal any sin in your own life that might prevent you from forgiving your mate (such as pride).
- Ask God for the wisdom to understand why your mate responded the way he did.
- Ask God for the wisdom to bring about the widest spiritual benefit from the situation.

TALK TO YOUR MATE ABOUT HOW HARD IT IS TO FORGIVE HIM

- Find a time and a place that is conducive to uninterrupted conversation (which might eliminate the checkout line at the supermarket, or a commercial break during the televised football game).
- Explain exactly what you are having trouble forgiving.
- Don't use emotion as your weapon; explain yourself with reason and compassion.

GIVE YOUR MATE A CHANCE TO RESPOND

- Don't put answers in his mouth.
- Give him time to think about what you've said. Remember you've been thinking about the problem for a long time, but it might be the first time your mate has known it to be a difficulty.
- Ask your mate for suggestions concerning ways you could get through this struggle.

PLAN A COURSE OF ACTION UPON WHICH YOU BOTH CAN AGREE

- If your mate asks for forgiveness, accept it without reservation.
- If your mate refuses to see that he has any personal blame in the situation (i.e., says "it's your problem"), then at least he knows what is bothering you and how you intend to handle it on your own.

SHOW YOUR MATE TOTAL FORGIVENESS

- If you say "I forgive you," mean it. Don't bring the offense up to him again; do not tell other people what he did—or didn't—do.
- Do not complain to God about something you said you have forgiven him for.
- Don't waste your time sitting around sulking about it to yourself.

LEAVE THE MATTER IN GOD'S HANDS

- God is in charge of securing justice, and He is much better at it than we are.
- If you think your mate is getting off better than he deserves, be careful about your prayers. Are you ready to get all that you deserve from the Lord?

SEEK THE LORD'S PERSPECTIVE OF THE OFFENSE

- Some offenses (unconfessed, continuing adultery, for one) are of major significance both to the Lord and to your marriage.

Obviously, you will need further leading from the Lord if this is
your case.
- Other failures (running over your favorite set of golf clubs, for
example) should be dealt with more quickly.

CLEAN THE CLOSET OF YOUR MIND OFTEN

- Old offenses have no place in your life. Even for serious crimes
there is a statute of limitations. If your mate did something
twenty years ago, two years ago, or two months ago, it should be
settled by now.
- It's best to deal with the offense on the very day you first notice
that you are having difficulty in forgiving it.

GIVE YOUR MATE THE CONSIDERATION YOU DEMAND OF HIM

We are prone to require more of others than we ourselves would
give to them.

How important is forgiveness in building friendship in marriage?
Ask our friend Stuart. He and Stella had been married thirty-five
years when a girl twenty years younger than Stuart made a pass at
him. Stuart surprised his wife, his grown kids, and even himself
when he ran off with his new-found sweetheart.

Stella was crushed. She tried to start life over. Fifty-eight is not
exactly the prime of life. She knew she still loved Stuart, but she
thought she could never forgive him. She was only half right. For the
next six years Stuart continued to run away from responsibility. He
tried to act thirty-five, well, at least forty-five. He knew he had made
the most horrible mistake of his life, but he was too ashamed to pre-
sume on Stella's forgiveness.

But Stella wasn't sitting still. She was a wise enough gal to know
that no matter what the future brought she had to learn to forgive
Stu. She did not want to spend the last years of her life as a bitter,
old woman. It took her some six years to work through it. There
were times of tears, doubts, and spiritual growth. Finally, she sent
Stu a Christmas card. It was the first positive communication in
years. At Easter she sent a card and a little note. Just a visit about
what she was doing.

On June 25, Stu showed up at her front door. It was her birthday. Sheepishly he admitted that he hadn't seen the other lady in five years, that he had often thought of Stella, and that he had behaved like an inexcusable jerk.

Stella nodded agreement.

On July 4, Stu asked Stella if she would like to go out for dinner at the Riverbend Lodge.

Stella nodded agreement.

On December 17, their original wedding date, Stu walked her back down an aisle and asked her to marry him.

Stella nodded agreement.

That was nine years ago this winter. We want to tell you that is one happy couple. We want to tell you there are three delighted children. We want to tell you there are eight thrilled grandchildren.

Not that it's been easy.

But they worked through the tough times together.

Sure, there's still plenty of forgiveness needed.

That's what best friends are for.

11

Developing a Spiritual Friendship

They may be the most widely known mother and father, husband and wife, in the history of the world.

They just might be the most important couple in the Bible. They certainly deserve the honor, though they didn't seem to get much respect while they were here on earth.

There was nothing about their background that hinted they would attain such prominence. They grew up in an obscure province of the Roman Empire. Their race was not highly esteemed. The city of their home was a long journey from the national capitol.

Oh, there was some royalty way back in their lineage. But that was way too far back to make any difference, or so they thought.

They planned their future together. Much like their parents before them, they expected long hours of hard work and life on a tight budget. But they would survive. They had each other and they both loved their God.

The engagement was announced. The wedding plans were made. Then came the shocker: the bride-to-be was pregnant. Her fiancé was not the father. Yet she claimed virginity and some story about a baby that would someday be Israel's Messiah.

Her husband-to-be bought the story.

Oh, people could laugh, scoff, or ridicule, but they had to admit that those two were in it together. They supported each other totally throughout the strange events of the birth of a son. If you pressed them, they would share incredible accounts of heavenly visions, choruses of angels, and wise men from the East. They stuck to their story, year after year. Whatever else we want to say about them, we cannot deny Mary and Joseph were a team. And they were the only couple on earth that the Almighty God ever entrusted with the care of His Son.

Joseph was a man of integrity and compassion. When he found out Mary was pregnant, he would not compromise biblical moral standards. He was a "righteous man, and not wanting to disgrace her, desired to put her away secretly" (Matthew 1:19). Joseph knew that he had every right to divorce Mary, but in his deep love for her he desired to put her away secretly, thus avoiding scandal. But Joseph was also obedient to his Lord. When an angel of the Lord appeared to him in a dream, saying, "Joseph, son of David, do not be afraid to take Mary as your wife; for that which has been conceived in her is of the Holy Spirit" (Matthew 1:20), Joseph obeyed. He "arose from his sleep, and did as the angel of the Lord commanded him, and took her as his wife" (Matthew 1:24).

Mary was a young lady of deep piety and devotion. Confronted by an angelic visitor with the most unusual message in Scripture, she simply said, "Behold, the bondslave of the Lord; be it done to me according to your word" (Luke 1:38).

We spend little time thinking about them, except at Christmas. It's Jesus who's important, we say. We're correct, of course. But consider their situation.

Joseph was forced to travel across the country to pay taxes right at the time his wife was ready to deliver a baby. Why did she travel with him? Weren't there any relatives in Nazareth to help out? Didn't they have at least some distant friends in Bethlehem to provide that customary Eastern hospitality?

No relatives to help. No friends to stand with them. Just a painfully pregnant young woman and a nervous husband, both extremely poor and far away from home. But they had a vision to share . . . a dream . . . a promise. They did not hesitate to devote themselves to their vision, no matter how long it took or how great the discomfort. Mary and Joseph remain for all time the prime example of a couple with a commitment to a spiritual friendship. Together they accomplished God's plan for their lives. There were no words of resentment. No shouts of anger. No expressions of bitterness. They faced their assignment with peace and trusted in a very personal God.

STRENGTHEN THE SPIRITUAL DIMENSION OF YOUR FRIENDSHIP

The spiritual dimension of the friendship you have with your mate needs to be built up and strengthened just as much as the emotional and physical dimensions. Like many positive things in marriage, strong spiritual friendships don't just happen.

How strong is your spiritual friendship?

- Suppose your non-Christian neighbor gives you a frantic phone call and wants you to drive her to the hospital with her three-year-old who has just accidently swallowed some poison. You stay by her side for six hours. You cry and pray and cry some more. But the little one dies. Your neighbor keeps asking you "Why? Why? How could God let this happen?" You have no easy answers. After you finally drive her back home, the one person you want to talk to is (a) your pastor? (b) your Christian friend across town? (c) your mate?
- Two neatly dressed young men appear at your front door asking you if they can visit with you about spiritual matters. They begin to quote from a book with which you are unfamiliar. You tell them you are a Christian and follow the Bible as your guide. They claim their book is just as authoritative as yours. You know that's not true, but you can't remember the chapters and verses which state that. As they drone on you say to yourself, "I sure wish (a) my pastor (b) my Christian friend across town (c) my mate was here."
- After church, two of the elders approach you with an opportunity to use your gifts and talents in a new ministry that is beginning in the church. It will take some time, but it offers a hopeful prospect of spiritual success. You feel that you just have to talk to somebody about it. Immediately you start to look around for (a) your pastor? (b) your Christian friend who knows you well? (c) your mate?

In a marriage with a strong spiritual friendship you will find yourself constantly reaching out for your mate's advice and support when you are confronted with tough spiritual situations.

No matter how strong the spiritual friendship might be, we need to continue to build unity and maturity. The quiz that follows can help. Take time to answer all these questions about your mate. When you have finished, have your mate jot down answers to all these questions about you. Then spend an evening sharing answers. Be open to learning from your mate's perception of your spiritual life. If he has missed some answers, help him out.

BE AWARE OF WHAT IS GOD DOING IN YOUR MATE'S LIFE

Answer the following about your mate:

1. What was his conversion experience? When and where did it occur? What were the circumstances of his first accepting Jesus Christ as Lord and Savior? In answering, try to use the sort of terms he would use to describe the experience.
2. Who is his hero from Scripture (other than Jesus)? Why?
3. What do you think are your mate's five strongest spiritual abilities?
4. Can you name three specific occasions in the past year where you assisted in strengthening his spiritual life?
5. Does he have a life (theme) verse from the Bible? Or a favorite verse? What is it? Where is it found? Why does he like that one so well?
6. What's the toughest part of your mate's spiritual life at this time? (What does he struggle with the most right now?)
7. What three items, besides family members, do you know for sure are on your mate's prayer list?
8. Which is your mate's favorite book in the Bible? Why do you think so?
9. What is your mate's most serious spiritual weakness?
10. When was the last time the two of you had a serious spiritual discussion that lasted over five minutes? What was it about? What was the outcome of the discussion?

Perhaps after working through questions like these, the two of you will want to continue working on building a spiritual friendship. Rather than just dreaming about what you might achieve one day, you can diligently apply yourself to building that element of your marriage right now. Here are a few places you might like to begin.

SUPPORT YOUR MATE'S SPIRITUAL COMMITMENT

ACCEPT YOUR MATE'S PRESENT SPIRITUAL STATE AS A STARTING POINT FOR GROWTH

Be realistic about your mate. Accept his present spiritual state as a satisfactory starting place for spiritual growth.

We discussed this subject a few chapters back when we talked about those who have an unspiritual mate. Let's emphasize the point again. So your husband may not be the guy over on Mountain View Circle. You know, the guy who teaches the Sunday school class, leads the youth club recreation on Tuesday nights, takes the junior highers backpacking every summer, is the star pitcher on the church softball team, fills in for the pastor when he's on vacation, and takes his wife out to a fancy restaurant every Friday night.

And your wife may not be the lead soprano in the choir, a concert violinist, the vacation Bible school director, a volunteer summer missionary in South America, and the author of a best-selling journal of theological essays—like the gal who lives in the big house just south of town.

Let your mate be himself. Whatever his spiritual maturity might be, it's an acceptable level for you to begin building a great spiritual friendship—one that is uniquely your own, unlike anyone else's. We all know how destructive it is to a relationship to always be comparing your mate's physical looks to others'. It's even worse to compare spiritual gifts and Christian maturity. There is no one on earth who looks exactly like your mate—physically or spiritually.

ACCEPT YOUR MATE'S SPIRITUAL GROWTH RATE

Accept your mate's growth rate even if it is different than yours. Don't insist that the two of you grow at exactly the same rate. It is always a joy and a delight for a couple to mature together in the Lord.

"What do you know about the Holy Ghost?"

"The what?"

"Not what, who."

"Who?"

"Yeah, who!"

Steve thought he was caught in the middle of an Abbott and Costello routine. We had been Christians a total of six months when Janet started reading about the power of the Holy Ghost in the lives of believers. We felt like the early Ephesians. Paul said to them, " 'Did you receive the Holy Spirit when you believed?' And they said to him, 'No, we have not even heard whether there is a Holy Spirit' " (Acts 19:2).

Imagine our delight to find out, indeed, we had the Holy Spirit of God dwelling in us. We grew quickly together as we learned more and more about His work in us. But simultaneous growth is not always the case in a marriage friendship.

For three years Steve attended seminary. Every day was a discovery of spiritual truth. His confidence and ability grew, and his gifts developed. Janet spent those three years working. There were kids to raise, bills to pay—not everyone can spend his days studying. Her growth was in different areas.

"I'll never get through Augustine!" Steve moaned.

"And I'll be lucky to get through August," Janet countered.

We've had some disagreements to work through when our spiritual lives seemed in conflict.

"Jan, I think the Lord wants us to move to rural northern Idaho," Steve announced one day.

"Funny," Janet shot back, "I was talking to Him this morning and He didn't say a thing about it to me."

Your spiritual growth will be that way throughout life. Sometimes slow, sometimes fast, sometimes together, sometimes alone. Let the Lord set the rate of growth in your life and in your mate's. If your mate is actively seeking to know and follow the Lord, his growth rate is in just the right areas, and at just the speed that He wants.

ENCOURAGE YOUR MATE TO AIM FOR SPIRITUAL GOALS

Most folks set goals for their lives. Usually these have to do with accomplishments we hope to achieve. "Someday, I'm going to own my own store." "By the time I'm forty, I'm going to own that cabin in the woods." "My goal is to be the leading lady in the community operetta." "I'm going to have enough money in the bank to retire at fifty-five." "Stick with me, kid, and I'll get you that condo by the lake." "It might take me twenty years, but I'm going to get that college degree."

But goals are also needed in the spiritual realm and they need to be biblically based, spiritual goals. These goals can be ones having to do with behavior and attitudes:

- "Be angry, and yet do not sin; do not let the sun go down on your anger" (Ephesians 4:26).
- "And whoever shall force you to go one mile, go with him two" (Matthew 5:41).
- "Do all things without grumbling or disputing" (Philippians 2:14).

Pick out weak areas in your own life, and find a Bible verse that, if applied, would overcome your weaknesses. Ask your mate to help you achieve those goals, and be appreciative when he gives you the assistance you need to achieve your goals.

Or they can be goals that define a whole life-style:

- "But prove yourselves doers of the word, not merely hearers who delude themselves" (James 1:22).
- "But seek first His kingdom and His righteousness; and all these things shall be added to you" (Matthew 6:33).
- "If anyone wishes to come after Me, let him deny himself, and take up his cross, and follow Me" (Mark 8:34).
- "Run in such a way that you may win" (1 Corinthians 9:24).

Select a verse to keep as your lifelong goal, or yearly goal, or even monthly goal. Share that verse with your mate. Ask him to memorize it with you and to use it to keep you aiming in the right direction.

Perhaps your goal is to model your life after a biblical character. Striving to be like Joshua, Daniel, John the Baptist, Paul, or Timothy is certainly a worthwhile spiritual aim. So is patterning your life after Sarah, Hannah, Martha, Lydia, or Priscilla.

Be your mate's number one helper in achieving his spiritual goals.

ENCOURAGE YOUR MATE'S AREAS OF SPIRITUAL STRENGTH

Keep emphasizing your mate's strong points. Sure, he has weaknesses, and sometimes they can drive you up a wall. But your mate also does some things well.

The kickback mate who refuses to take his turn leading the weekly home Bible study just might be a great, patient listener to whom everybody wants to talk because "he always seems to understand just how I feel."

The timid wife who refuses to travel with you on the spring break mission trip to Mexico loves having company and is never flustered when you invite someone home after church.

We all have some spiritual strengths. Let your mate know how much you appreciate those abilities.

And learn from your mate.

The very best teacher you have for spiritual truth (in addition to your children) is your mate. He knows you best . . . and he spends more time around you than anyone else does. The Lord will certainly use him to teach you a few things.

"I'm glad I have you around . . . I'm not very spiritually discerning."

"Hey, would you read these verses for me? I'm having a hard time figuring them out."

"Did you notice that something's wrong with Martin? You always sense things like that better than I do."

Consider you and your mate to be a spiritual team. If you don't take advantage of both members' skills, it's a cinch you will have a losing season.

AGREE ON THE IMPORTANCE OF A SPIRITUAL GOAL
IN RELATION TO FAMILY PRIORITIES

You and your spouse need to agree on the relative importance of an individual goal in the light of family priorities. Don't make your mate feel as though time spent on his or her individual spiritual growth is a detriment to family life. A spiritually strong and healthy family is made up of spiritually strong and healthy individuals.

Send your wife to the women's retreat as you volunteer to keep the kids. Let your husband take the Bible school course by correspondence, even if you can't buy the new drapes this year.

Mom can't go to every conference. Dad can't take every course. But make sure your mate knows that you think his individual growth opportunities are important.

In 1974, Steve sent Janet off on a bus to a "Christian Writer's Conference." She was gone six days during Easter week and he had charge of a ten- and seven-year-old, as well as pastoring a church. The food wasn't as tasty that week. The boys' hair didn't get washed as well. The house was somewhat messier and the hugs not nearly as tender, but Mom needed that time.

She didn't write anything in '74, but he sent her off again in '75 and '76. Then together, the Blys began to write an article here and a story there and a few poems. Then one day, along came a book. By '89 there were nearly four hundred articles, plays, poems, short stories, and radio scripts . . . not to mention nineteen books—and a calling into a full-time writing and speaking ministry together.

It all started with a couple who realized the importance of each other's individual spiritual growth.

BE ALERT TO OPPORTUNITIES TO MINISTER TOGETHER

Be on the lookout for opportunities and projects of mutual ministry. This is something we mentioned earlier, but it bears repeating. You will find great times of building spiritual friendship when you minister and serve together.

You might enjoy the same ministries.

Every Tuesday night for the past six years Tony and Liza have gone out visiting new people who attend their church. They love talking with people and offering their help. But not every couple feels comfortable doing that together.

Brenda would be too petrified for such a venture. Of course, her husband Richard could do it—he's so outgoing and friendly even the animals visit with him! But we haven't seen Richard and Brenda for over four months. They went off to the Sudan to work at a mission station. Can you imagine two people, aged forty-five, just leaving home like that? Brenda's teaching missionary children, and Richard's building a Bible school when he isn't visiting with the locals about the Lord.

That's what ministry together is all about. Not both doing the identical thing, necessarily, but working together for the same goal.

PUBLICLY SUPPORT WHAT GOD IS DOING IN YOUR MATE'S LIFE

Find a way to publicly support what God is doing in your mate's life. Your mate has some faults and some weaknesses. Some of those will be seen publicly; some will be hidden. It is not your calling in life to expose all your mate's mistakes to the world. The Lord has plenty of other ways of doing that. If you want to build a solid, spiritual friendship, make your public declarations about your mate positive statements about spiritual strengths.

Be honest. She might not have the most perfect voice in the world, but she might have ministered in a powerful way to someone through a solo. Let her, and others, know that you're proud.

He's not exactly Billy Graham when it comes to convicting messages, but did you see the way those two high schoolers hung on his every word when he told them about his conversion during the war? Let him know you noticed. It's O.K. if others hear you confirm him.

SPEND ONE HALF-HOUR TOGETHER EVERY DAY FOR NINETY DAYS

If you are serious about really beginning to build a spiritual friendship, find time to spend one half-hour together every day for ninety days.

Pledge to spend:

- ten minutes reading Scripture out loud, together
- ten minutes listening to each other's spiritual joys and struggles (five minutes for each mate)
- ten minutes sharing prayer requests and praying for each other

For some, making room for this time together sounds like an impossible task. But we guarantee that it's worth every effort it takes.

Look around at your Christian friends and you will begin to find some really good marriages. Many have been working hard over the years to become their mate's best friend.

But keep on looking at those couples, and here and there, every once in a while, you will find a truly great marriage. Without fail you'll find the difference is the fact that that couple has discovered what spiritual friendship truly means.

12

Calling Your Mate to Account

Maybe they were too friendly. That is, if friendly means just going
along with whatever your mate wants. He always agreed with her.
She always agreed with him. Their continual harmony cost them
dearly.

Some pretty impressive things were going on in their church. People
were getting saved and suddenly were living completely changed
lives. The cruel became compassionate. The rebellious became law-
abiding. The greedy became generous.

Then a man from the islands accepted the Lord and decided to sell
a big piece of land and give all the money to the church board to
help with the ministry. It was impressive. His generosity had everyone talking. It even encouraged some to copy his example. Well,
sort of.

One particular couple thought to themselves, "Wouldn't it be
nice to have everyone in the church be as impressed with our generosity?" So they decided to sell their place and give the money to the
church. But somewhere in the planning of things they developed res-
ervations. We can imagine all sorts of doubts creeping in.

"What if we have some emergency needs next year? What would
we do for money?"

"Can we know for sure that the church leaders will use the funds
wisely? We wouldn't want them to fritter it away."

"There are a few nice things we could purchase. We've worked hard all these years; we deserve to enjoy some of our success."

"We'd better be considering the kids and the grandkids. We don't want to waste all their inheritance."

Besides that, they must have gotten a very good price for the property. That's what prompted the little scheme. They sold the place, then decided to tell the church board that they had actually sold it for a smaller amount and they wanted to give all the money from the sale to the church, just like the other man. After all, who would know? They would receive all the acclaim for being generous, and yet hold onto a nice, little nest egg for themselves.

Who says you can't have it all?

The Lord . . . that's who.

The story of Ananias and Sapphira is found in Acts 5:1-11.

When the husband, Ananias, brought the money to the church leaders, claiming it was the entire amount of the sale, Peter replied: "Ananias, why has Satan filled your heart to lie to the Holy Spirit, and to keep back some of the price of the land? While it remained unsold, did it not remain your own? And after it was sold, was it not under your control? Why is it that you have conceived this deed in your heart? You have not lied to men, but to God" (Acts 5:3-4).

Ananias did not take this public humiliation well. "And as he heard these words, Ananias fell down and breathed his last" (Acts 5:5).

Well, a few hours later the wife, Sapphira, showed up at the church. She didn't know anything had gone wrong. We suppose she might have been busy down at the local mall spending some of that excess money. When Peter confronted her to see if she was in on the charade, she fell for his trap.

"Then Peter said to her, 'Why is it that you have agreed together to put the Spirit of the Lord to the test? Behold, the feet of those who have buried your husband are at the door, and they shall carry you out as well.' And she fell immediately at his feet, and breathed her last" (Acts 5:9-10).

Peter said they had "agreed together." That sounds like a nice, friendly thing to do.

They were a couple with good communication skills. A couple who liked to do things together. But they were also a couple with an extremely important element of friendship missing. That missing element, which literally cost them their lives, was this: good friends are willing to confront one another.

We do this in some areas. We don't hesitate to tell our mate quietly:

"Dear, your fly is unzipped."

"Honey, your slip is showing."

"Sweetie, you've got huckleberries stuck on your teeth."

"Lambie-pie, there's a dryer cloth sticking out from under your blouse."

If we are so concerned about appearances, why don't we act as concerned about our mate's spiritual condition? One reason might be that we can't see how we can confront and still remain friends. Spiritual lives are delicate. Anyway, who are we to challenge someone else's spiritual life? It leaves us wide open for the same medicine.

Yet if we don't confront, who will? God has placed us with our particular mate for precisely that reason. If you are to help your mate become all that the Lord wants him to be, you have an obligation to call him to account.

How to Deal with Your Mate's Spiritual Failures

BEFORE THE CONFRONTATION

Before the confrontation occurs, you can be working toward a solution.

Demonstrate your loyalty. Don't assume it is your spiritual duty to correct your mate, especially after twenty-five years of constant nagging, complaining, and picking away at his dreams and goals. If that has been your pattern, he will view you as an enemy and anything you say in the present will be perceived as just the latest attack in an ongoing war.

Start to look for ways to prove that you are really on his side. If your mate believes that he suffered some injustice at work, take his side. Let your mate know you will support him, whatever action he chooses to take.

He: I'm so mad about being bypassed for the promotion I feel like quitting.
She: You're right. They shouldn't treat you that way. Why don't you quit. You're a good worker; you can land another job.
He: What about income?
She: Hey, we'll make it. You just shouldn't have to face that every morning of the week.

Loyalty, especially if it's been neglected, is not established overnight. But it does grow. And it builds confidence in the relationship. Everyone needs to know there is one person on the face of this earth he can turn to and absolutely count on to be on his side and to have his best interest in mind.

Remember also that loyalty is best built long before confrontation is needed. So if your mate seems to be sailing along in his spiritual life, now is the time to weave even more closely the bonds of loyalty. You will be more helpful to your mate later on.

Demonstrate your own spiritual growth. Part of building a proper relationship that will survive future confrontations is to show your growing spiritual maturity. Be serious about pushing for personal spiritual growth.

Greg is a quiet Christian guy. He never seems pushy but steadily charts his own course and follows his own plan. He was a Christian several years before his wife accepted the Lord.

Terri told us, "Greg never pushed anything on me. For years I waited for him to shove this religion thing at me. Then I was going to crucify him with his past. I mean, Greg used to be pretty wild, you know?

"Well, I'd get up in the morning and Greg would be at the counter eating his cereal and reading a Bible. He used to close it up when I walked in and visit with me. After a year or so of his closing it up, I figured it didn't hurt to ask what he'd been reading. From time to time I'd ask about the reading and he'd tell me a little more about the Bible. Anyway, one thing lead to another and before long, I was in church and went to the altar to accept the Lord.

"Even after that, I'd listen to Greg as he stopped to visit with the pastor after church about the sermon. It seemed like Greg always got more out of it than I did. But I don't remember his ever complaining about me being so dumb. Well, there was one time," Terri paused, "I decided not to send my Dad a Christmas card anymore. He had refused to attend our wedding, and in our five years of marriage he had never sent a letter, present, or card. But Greg wouldn't let me give up. He showed me some Scripture about honoring your father and your mother and I realized I needed to keep working at it.

"But it wasn't as if he was shoving it down my throat. It's just that I know I can trust Greg's spiritual advice. He works hard to understand what God wants us to do. I'd really like to be more like Greg myself."

Demonstrate your vulnerability. Long before there is ever a confrontation, let your mate know that you in no way think that you're perfect. Let him see that you are working on overcoming your own faults. Each of us has his own areas of weaknesses that cry out to be strengthened. That's where to begin.

If you honestly don't know what you should be working on, ask your mate to give you some suggestions.

Our friend Kelly had a problem with watching soap operas. It started out with one, then two, then four. Two hours a day, five days a week. They left her depressed, drained, and way behind on other things she wanted to accomplish.

"Ray, those soap operas take up my time and they tie up my emotions. I've got to stop," she announced one day.

It wasn't that easy. They tried unplugging the set, calling Ray at work, and a monetary fine. Finally, Ray built a beautiful wood stereo center where he could close a door on the television and lock it. Kelly broke the habit she wanted broken, and they both rejoiced.

Last month Kelly was shocked when a copy of a men's magazine arrived in the mail. The costumes the ladies wore in the pictures were scantier than the meager content of the articles. She confronted Ray. He said some guy at work had subscribed to it for all the fellows because his ex-girlfriend's picture was on the cover.

"Besides," Ray said, "sometimes the articles are helpful."

"For what!" Kelly questioned, "Don't you think this is just as potentially harmful for you as the soap operas were for me?"

"Yeah," Ray conceded, "you've got a point."

The magazine was tossed and the subscription junked. "What with Kelly working so hard on some things in her life," Ray told us, "I needed to push a little harder to keep up."

DURING THE CONFRONTATION

As children of God, we must be rebuked for unrepented sins. "Be on your guard! If your brother sins, rebuke him" (Luke 17:3).

A rebuke, by its nature, is a sharp criticism. You can't rebuke without letting the other one know that he is doing something wrong. It will catch your mate by surprise, either because he does not recognize his problem, or because he has purposely chosen to ignore it.

Why do we ever think that someone else should rebuke our mate? Do we really want to wait until the whole neighborhood, the whole church, the whole town knows about his failures?

But when you rebuke, make sure you help him understand that what you are concerned about is not just something you do not like but is something unbiblical. You might want to have the biblical teaching on the subject ready, just in case your mate needs more convincing.

The rebuke shouldn't stop there. You should be committed to more than just a verbal assault. You want to let your mate know that you are ready to help him find a corrective to the problem as well.

The rebuke should come with patience and instruction. "Preach the word; be ready in season and out of season; reprove, rebuke, exhort, with great patience and instruction" (2 Timothy 4:2).

Patience . . . the ability to change the present situation but refusing to do so because you believe holding back will produce a better result. Yes, you could be more graphic in your rebuke. Yes, you could try to repay the pain and anguish your mate has put you through. Yes, you could lay down a "straighten-out-or-else" ultimatum. But you don't. That's patience.

You can yell at a little kid, "Don't play with matches!" Or you can take the child aside and explain in some detail where playing with matches often leads. The goal is the same. The difference is instruction. The better the instruction, the better the success ratio.

Demonstrate that it's not a problem you are expecting your spouse to face alone. "Brethren, even if a man is caught in any trespass, you who are spiritual, restore such a one in a spirit of gentleness; each one looking to yourself, lest you too be tempted. Bear one another's burdens, and thus fulfill the law of Christ" (Galatians 6:1-2).

What are the burdens we should be bearing?

The burdens of one another's sins.

Don't tell your mate, "Boy, you've got a problem and you better do something about it."

That's like saying to your partner as you float down the river in a two-person inflatable raft, "You've got a hole in your end of the boat; you'd better get busy and fix it."

When the boat fills up, everyone sinks.

When your mate fails to face his sin and repent, the whole marriage can collapse.

But confront him with gentleness. A gentle person always knows just the right time—and the wrong time—to get angry. He has a good sense of just how important the issue is and will not make the mistake of blowing things out of proportion.

Don't make enemies with your mate. "And yet do not regard him as an enemy, but admonish him as a brother" (2 Thessalonians 3:15).

It should not be your goal in life to constantly put your mate in his place. Confronting a mate is always done for the purpose of uniting a couple, rather than pushing them apart. Sometimes there is a momentary recoil as your mate considers your complaint. But the purpose remains—to make our marriage stronger.

An enemy is one who is actively working against your best interest. It is important in times of confrontation in one area that you make sure there are others areas of life in which you solidly support your mate.

"Man, you are always on my case about something. What do I ever have to do to please you?"

These are words spoken to a supposed enemy, not a best friend. In fact, think about the words you choose, the tone of your voice, and its volume. If someone in the other room heard you, would they know that you were confronting your lifetime mate, lover, and very best friend? Or would they think you were telling off the latest tele-marketing pest?

Make sure your confrontation passes the wisdom test. In our book *How to Be a Good Mom* (Chicago: Moody, 1988) we mention that one way we can know if our words agree with the Lord's will is if they meet the criteria of James 3:17: "But the wisdom from above is first pure, then peaceable, gentle, reasonable, full of mercy and good fruits, unwavering, without hypocrisy."

Think over what you have to say.

- Does it come from a sincere motive of love?
- Does it have as its long-range goal the restoring of peace in the marriage?
- Is it based on an angry reaction?
- Are you making an effort to show mercy?
- Will the spiritual result you envision please God?
- Is it exactly the way you would want to be treated if the roles were reversed?
- Do you have a hidden agenda for bringing the matter up? Is there a possibility that your concern over your spouse's faults is a smoke screen to cover up your own failings?

Take time to consider the exact words you use in the confrontation. Remember the old backyard chant, "Sticks and stones can break my bones but words will never harm me"?

It's a lie.

Words cripple, maim, paralyze, and even kill. Choose the words of confrontation carefully.

"Let no unwholesome word proceed from your mouth, but only such a word as is good for edification according to the need of the moment, that it may give grace to those who hear" (Ephesians 4:29).

Choose words that will help your mate gain spiritual knowledge, that will help him understand the grace of God. Let him be reminded of God's love and forgiveness.

Paul says in Colossians 4:6, "Let your speech always be with grace, seasoned, as it were, with salt, so that you may know how you should respond to each person."

Seasoned with salt. Salt is used to retard spoilage and bring out the flavor. The right words of rebuke can stop your mate's slide away from obedience to the Lord, and in speaking them you can help him enjoy more fully the rich blessings of life the Lord has in store for all His children.

AFTER THE CONFRONTATION

The fact that you survived the confrontation itself does not mean your work is complete. Remember, your mate is still sifting through the aftermath.

Allow your mate to suffer the consequences. "Do not be deceived, God is not mocked; for whatever a man sows, this he will also reap" (Galatians 6:7).

Sin costs. The price is often extremely expensive. You might be able to minimize the cost, but you will never be able to eliminate it. In fact, you shouldn't even try.

Many of the consequences of sin are God's object lessons given to discourage a repeat of such behavior.

Give your mate enough time for repentance to do its full work. Seldom do mates rejoice at having sin openly displayed. We all have different patterns of acceptance.

King David instantly confessed, "I have sinned against the Lord" (2 Samuel 12:13), when he was confronted with his sins of adultery and murder.

Peter's denial of knowing Jesus in Mark 14:66-72 created long-lasting guilt in him. In fact, it was not until many days after the resurrection that the situation was finally resolved by the Lord's repeated question, "Do you love Me?" (John 21:15-17)

Give your mate a reasonable amount of time to respond to your confrontation.

Rejoice together in every confrontation that you have worked through. Surviving a serious confrontation in marriage can be a tremendous milestone to pass: "If we could work through that, we can work through anything!"

The strongest marriages have worked through some serious challenges. If you haven't, you are probably still wondering just how secure your marriage really is. For the past dozen years new buildings constructed in southern California have been required to meet "earthquake proof" standards. The problem is, there has not yet been a sufficient earthquake to properly test their strength.

Don't go out and look for problems in your marriage, but if a serious confrontation is unavoidable, consider the possibility that it might be the Lord's way to let you know just how strong, or weak, your friendship really is.

Remember Ananias and Sapphira? A sad story. We wish we could rewrite the script.

Ananias:	Sapphie, honey, the real estate agent called and some rich dude from Egypt offered us ninety thousand shekels for our little rental down on 45th Street.
Sapphira:	Ninety thousand! It's not worth half that.
Ananias:	I guess he's going to put in a little milk and honey fast food place. Anyway, the guy's loaded . . . a perfume merchant, I guess.
Sapphira:	What will we do with all that money?
Ananias:	Listen, little pomegranate, remember all the fuss over Barney when he donated all the money from the sale of his place?
Sapphira:	It's still the talk of the church.
Ananias:	I've got a great plan . . . see, we tell the church board that we sold the place for fifty thousand, that's more than it's worth, and we can just pocket the rest. What do you think?
Sapphira:	Wow, Ananie, all that money is tempting, and we could sure have some fun spending it, but . . . well . . . you know . . . it just wouldn't be honest. I suppose the Lord would rather we give to His work out of our desire to give, instead of to achieve status or fame. I say we tithe it right away, and then put the rest in the bank and pray about what God would have us do.

Ananias: Oh, Sapphie, my precious jewel, once again wisdom has dripped from your ruby lips. Let's do as you said. How could I ever get along without your sweet counsel?

We wish we could rewrite the story of Ananias and Sapphira. It would have saved their witness, their integrity, and their lives. But it's too late for them.

But not for you. Honest, loving, forgiving confrontation can still purify your marriage. You still have plenty of time to prove that you really are your mate's best friend.

13

Friends and Partners

They were the ones who should have written this book. They had the background and the experience of no other couple in the Bible. Mentioned six times in Scripture, they are never introduced separately. Twice the husband's name is listed first; four times the wife's. But it doesn't matter. No one ever thought of them as anything other than a team.

Aquila and his wife, Priscilla (or Prisca), rule without debate as the Bly's favorite couple in Scripture.

We first learn about them in Acts 18:2-3. Paul had traveled to Europe for the first time, and after taking the gospel to Macedonia, preaching at the Areopagus in Athens, he entered the wild peninsula town of Corinth.

"And he found a certain Jew name Aquila, a native of Pontus, having recently come from Italy with his wife Priscilla, because Claudius had commanded all the Jews to leave Rome. He came to them, and because he was of the same trade, he stayed with them and they were working; for by trade they were tent-makers" (Acts 18:2-3).

We know nothing about their conversion to Christ. But we know that when the gospel exploded into the Roman Empire at Pentecost, the words of testimony reached out to the farthest reaches of civilization. Luke records that there were "visitors from Rome, both Jews and proselytes" (Acts 2:10). Perhaps it was through visitors to Jerusalem on Pentecost Day that Aquila and Priscilla first heard about Christ.

They were not natives of Rome. The Acts passage mentions the region of Pontus on the south shores of what we now call the Black Sea as their place of origin. And even if they were converted to Christ in Rome, they faced the same persecution as other Jews. In the early days, Christianity was regarded as a branch of Judaism by the Roman authorities.

Aquila and Priscilla headed east to the Achaia region of Greece and moved into the port city, Corinth, a wealthy commercial center. It was a huge city (it had a theater that seated 20,000) known for its fast money and wicked behavior.

Even in work, Aquila and Priscilla were partners. Paul joined the firm of Aquila and Priscilla to make tents to supply his income. Every good Jewish father taught his sons a trade, even if he later sent them to receive training in law and religion, like Paul. Having left his other friends behind in Athens, Paul must have been delighted to enter the city of Corinth and run across a couple of Christian tentmakers, who threw open their home and their business to him.

Just how valuable they were in Paul's ministry could be seen eighteen months later when he left the fledgling church for a new ministry.

"And Paul, having remained many days longer, took leave of the brethren and put out to sea for Syria, and with him were Priscilla and Aquila" (Acts 18:18).

In biblical times it is always significant when the wife's name is mentioned at all. We know that Peter traveled with his wife ("Do we not have a right to take along a believing wife, even as the rest of the apostles, and the brothers of the Lord, and Cephas [Peter]?" [1 Corinthians 9:5]), yet we are never told her name. But not so here —Paul just couldn't think of Aquila without mentioning Priscilla.

As Paul returned to his home church in Antioch of Syria, he stopped for a few days in the Asia Minor city of Ephesus. Some of the folks pleaded for Paul to stay in Ephesus, but he did not consent (Acts 18:19-20). So he did the next best thing. Paul left his good friends Priscilla and Aquila to minister to the believers in Ephesus.

We assume they continued their tentmaking and began to develop a new church in their home. That was their pattern everywhere they lived. But their authority and spiritual gifts went even deeper.

Acts 18:24-28 describes a powerful Christian preacher named Apollos who came to Ephesus. He's described as an "eloquent" man "mighty in the Scriptures" (v. 24), "instructed in the way of the Lord" (v. 25), "fervent in spirit" (v. 25), speaking "boldly" (v. 26).

In spite of all this, Apollos displayed an obvious flaw: his theology was incomplete. So when he showed up with his message at the synagogue in Ephesus, Priscilla and Aquila "took him aside and explained to him the way of God more accurately" (v. 26).

The spiritual maturity of the couple is obvious. They not only knew the more complete theology; they knew how to correct Apollos without publicly crushing him. "They took him aside." It wasn't just Aquila who knew the theology. It was that ministering couple, the spiritual partners, the best friends . . . Priscilla and Aquila.

Armed now with more perfect Christian teaching, Apollos wanted to push on and minister in Achaia (Athens and Corinth). Priscilla and Aquila "encouraged him and wrote to the disciples to welcome him" (v. 27).

When Apollos walked into the Christian fellowship at Corinth with letters of recommendation from Priscilla and Aquila, the congregation was going to listen.

So far, we see this couple as business partners of Paul's, as gracious folks with an obvious gift of hospitality, as exhorters, as encouragers, as willing missionaries, and as students of theology. But that's not all we hear of them.

In 1 Corinthians 16:19, when Paul concludes his letter to the huge and troubled church at Corinth he mentions some old friends they would all recognize. "The churches of Asia greet you. Aquila and Prisca greet you heartily in the Lord, with the church that is in their house."

Aquila and Prisca still had their eyes and their hearts bent toward Corinth. Notice, as always, there was a church meeting in their house. Remember, Christians in those early days had no buildings in which to meet, so any believers with a fairly large living room would volunteer to help. Wherever Prisca and Aquila went, their home was available for the Lord's work.

But though Ephesus was a main concern of this couple, they ministered in other regions as well. About two years later Paul wrote to believers in the great city of Rome, telling of his desire to come and be with them. After a deep theological discourse, Paul greeted those he knew were in the capital city.

"Greet Prisca and Aquila, my fellow workers in Christ Jesus, who for my life risked their own necks, to whom not only do I give thanks, but also all the other churches of the Gentiles; also greet the church that is in their house" (Romans 16:3-4). Perhaps the earlier religious persecutions in Rome had subsided for the time being,. so the industrious couple had returned. They were not called mere helpers, but "fellow workers," those who labored alongside Paul.

But this passage teaches us even more about them. Paul said that they (again, both of them) risked their lives for him. On just which of Paul's narrow escapes from death they assisted him, we are not told. It might have been a scene like the one in Ephesus (recorded in Acts 19:23-40), where a riot broke out in opposition to Paul's teaching. Wherever it was, this Christian couple put themselves between Paul and his attackers, willing to sacrifice their lives if that was called for.

Just how many couples do you suppose Paul knew who would have been willing to do that? Just how many couples do you know who would be willing to do the same thing for you? Well, Paul notes in Roman 16 that such a deed can never be properly repaid. Both he and all the churches that benefited from his ministry gave thanks to God for what Priscilla and Aquila had been willing to do.

There is one more chapter in their life. Paul says in his very last letter, "Greet Prisca and Aquila" (2 Timothy 4:19).

Eight years after writing to the Christians in Rome, the aged missionary, evangelist, church planter, and world-class theologian, now imprisoned and condemned to die, wrote to his spiritual son Timothy back in Ephesus. Paul knew his ministry was over: "I have fought the good fight, I have finished the course, I have kept the faith" (2 Timothy 4:7).

When he comes down to the last four lines he will ever write, he says, "Greet Prisca and Aquila." When Paul looked back over years of ministry, he couldn't forget their support and faithfulness.

Once again they had left Rome. They had returned to the region of Ephesus. Paul did not mention the church in their home, but he could have. Even though he was separated from his friends by thousands of miles, he knew they were working side by side. He could probably imagine them making tents, supporting the Christian ministry, inviting in traveling preachers, holding church meetings in their house, correcting errant theology, and putting their lives on the line for their faith.

Not merely a man.

Not merely a woman.

Not merely a man and his wife.

But, Priscilla and Aquila. Ministry partners . . . business partners . . . spiritual partners . . . best friends.

If we had a picture of them, we'd have it hanging in a prominent place for inspiration. If they'd written an autobiography, it surely would be the most worn volume in any Christian couple's library.

In a way, of course, Priscilla and Aquila are still teaching all of us who struggle to find the Lord's calling as couples. They remind us that what we seek is possible to find. Others have built the kind of relationship we hope to build. It can be done.

We can learn much from what is said about them.

- Neither husband nor wife felt it necessary to be identified by himself or herself.
- Both saw their entire lives and work as available to promote the Lord's kingdom.
- Both shared the labor, from tentmaking to theological instruction.
- Both were willing to set aside personal peace and ease and move to another location, if needed, for ministry.
- Both seemed always to keep in mind the larger goal of reaching more folks with the gospel.

They are the role models of intimate team ministry.

TEN GUIDELINES FOR MINISTRY TOGETHER

If you are serious about desiring to be best friends *and* ministry partners with your mate, you will need to review these points:

1. *Recognize and accept your mate's natural talents, acquired skills, and special spiritual gifts.* Minimize your mate's failures, and concentrate on understanding his strengths.

2. *Recognize and accept your mate's unique way of using those talents, skills, and gifts.* Even if the two of you have several skills in the same areas, one spouse might well use those skills in a different manner. Your spouse's gift of teaching and your gift of teaching might not look anything alike in practice. And his gift of teaching might not look like anyone else's either.

3. *Keep searching for opportunities for service that combine both of your talents, skills, and spiritual gifts.* Go to your pastor, church board, Christians friends, or Sunday school class and find out what ministries are available. Find at least one ministry together that excites both of you.

4. *Allow your mate some growing room.* Even ministry partners are not identical twins spiritually. Look for ways to encourage your mate to grow in his spiritual ministry. Give him books, send him to conferences, let him have time to explore the avenues that the Lord provides. Those opportunities do not need to destroy your ministry together, but rather they can help to define it, as each of you becomes confident of what the Lord wants you to do.

5. *Use your individual gifts privately to strengthen one another.* If you have the gift of teaching, then your mate has his own private teacher. If he has the gift of exhortation, then you will always have someone around to pick you up and help you get going again. And it's a wonderful thing to have your own private counselor or evangelist.

6. *Once you find a ministry you are both excited about, make it a high priority.* A high priority is something you will not put aside easily.

Our time gets pushed, shoved, stolen, and crowded. So we find ourselves swamped, even with Christian projects. That's when we need to cut back on some things. But don't back away from your ministry together.

7. *Avoid being competitive.* You don't have to be known by more folks in church than your husband. You don't have to sing solos better than your wife. You don't have to see who can spend the most time at committee meetings. If your spouse is having a successful ministry, you do not need to enter the same thing and prove that you can do it just as well. Keep remembering: you are on the same side.

8. *Keep your mate constantly updated on your spiritual growth and struggles.* When you are spiritual partners, there may be a tendency to bypass some things that you do not understand, because you assume your mate knows what's going on. But your mate may not know either. He may be just as confused as you are. If things are confusing, say so. If you are frustrated, blurt it out. If you are about to sink in the present situation, call for help.

9. *Pray daily together about your ministry opportunities.* There are the special unique opportunities to serve the Lord you would never have if the two of you weren't married. Let's face it, you might still sing in the choir or be an usher on Sunday morning no matter who you were married to. But you say, "If it weren't for my mate, I'd never even attempt to. . . ." Now, that task is one of your special team ministry opportunities.

10. *Trust God to bring something greater out of the two of you working together than He could ever accomplish through just one of you.* How thrilling it must be for the Father of all believers, and the Creator of all life, to look down and see us thoroughly enjoying our life and ministry together. That's what He had in mind in the first place. Now you can tackle some projects for Him that would frighten you away if you had to face them on your own. You have a best friend —who just happens to be your spiritual partner.

A whole book about being a best friend to your mate? Isn't that overkill? In a world filled with problems, is it that important?

It is to us.

Janet decided to spend the summer of 1985 at our home in Idaho. It is spacious, cool, and extremely quiet compared to the noisy hustle of pastoral life in southern California. She and Aaron would go north in early June and Steve would join them in August. That meant seven weeks of being apart.

Sure, there would be some strain, but we weren't newlyweds. Over twenty years of marriage had given us the confidence and security in the relationship necessary to survive the separation.

It worked out just fine . . . sort of. Janet had time to write, relax, and be with Aaron. Steve had no household confusion as he pushed on with a busy schedule at the church. We were able to tolerate the lack of physical affection (just barely) for that length of time. It was a good time for personal growth . . . or so we thought.

That logic impressed us so well that we tried another bout in the summer of 1986. We repeated the schedule and sent Janet north. Once again we made it through without any serious damage to our relationship.

But sometime during the second summer the foolishness of it all hit us. Sure, you can pump up your mental, physical, and spiritual strength to survive. But why play a survival game if you don't have to? What we each discovered at the same time was that we could get along without another adult in the house. We could change the sheets and the tires without someone else's help. With the right frame of mind and the right know-how we could perform just about everything our mate did.

If so, then why did we resolve never to do it again voluntarily?

Because seven weeks without your lover is a piece of cake compared to seven weeks without your best friend.

Steve had trouble with a lady at church, but there was no one to talk with about it.

Janet saw a fantastic meteorite shower, but it was flat with no one around to share it.

Steve had a great new book idea, but he lost it somewhere between Wednesday and Sunday.

Janet panicked when Aaron ripped open his knee, and she missed having someone around to drive to the doctor's with them.

Steve finally had some time to just sit at home and relax, but the empty house bored him to tears.

Janet had weeks and weeks to write but no one to help her generate characterizations.

Steve had to decide about the September preaching schedule with no private counselor to consult.

Janet listened to seven sermons but wasn't sure how to apply the messages.

No person on earth, no activity in the world, no invention of technology can take the place of having your best friend in the whole wide world right there by your side.

That is God's goal for every marriage.

You can be your mate's best friend.

Topical Index

Moody Press, a ministry of the Moody Bible Institute, is designed for education, evangelization, and edification. If we may assist you in knowing more about Christ and the Christian life, please write us without obligation: Moody Press, c/o MLM, Chicago, Illinois 60610.